THE TECHNIQUE OF
MARQUETRY

Canterbury Pilgrims. *Probably the largest marquetry panel ever made, 24 ft × 20 ft, designed by George Ramon and executed by Mr A Dunn, it was installed in the liner the S.S.* Queen Elizabeth *in the 1930s. (Photo: Stewart Bale)*

THE TECHNIQUE OF
MARQUETRY

By Marie Campkin

B. T. BATSFORD LIMITED

To Jurek

Acknowledgment

It would have been impossible to write this book without drawing on the experience of the many members of the Marquetry Society from whom I gained my knowledge of the craft, both through personal contact and through their writings in *The Marquetarian* magazine. Some of them have invented new techniques to apply to the craft; some have rediscovered or adapted old ones; all have been generous in sharing their experience. I would again like to acknowledge the help of present members of the Marquetry Society in bringing up to date some of the information in this book for its second edition. whose special methods I have described in the book: Mr J. Byrne, for methods of geometrical marquetry, Mr A. Ephrat for portraiture, Mr R. Wilcocks for dyeing of veneers, Mr A. Vigus for miniatures, and Messrs P. Jobling and S. Murrell for hints and tips on a variety of marquetry techniques.

I am also grateful to Mr W. Lincoln for information contained in his publications *Wood Technology* and *The Veneer Craftsman's Manual* to which I have made reference.

Photographs 23c, 76 and 107 are by Pace Photographers, Sidcup, Kent, and the remainder, unless otherwise indicated, are taken by Stanley Turek. The diagrams are by Jurek Pomianowski.

Finally, I should like to express particular thanks to Mr S. Murrell for kindly reading the manuscript and making some most helpful criticisms.

© *Marie Campkin 1969*
First published as Introducing Marquetry *in 1969*

ISBN 0 7134 2423 0 (hardback)
ISBN 0 7134 4624 2 (paperback)

Filmset by Keyspools Ltd, Golborne, Lancashire
Printed and bound in Great Britain by
Anchor Brendon Ltd, Tiptree, Essex
for the Publishers
B. T. Batsford Limited,
4 Fitzhardinge Street, London, W1H 0AH

Contents

Introduction

Marquetry is derived from the ancient craft of intarsia, the creation of patterns and designs by the inlaying of different kinds of solid wood into a background. In marquetry the designs are overlaid rather than inlaid, and made up from thin wood veneers, available in a great variety of colour and texture, by techniques requiring the simplest of tools yet offering unlimited scope for artistry and craftsmanship.

The present day marquetry enthusiast can derive inspiration from the work of craftsmen of the past—from the great marquetry furniture of the eighteenth century to the decorative panelling of the luxury liners in the 1930s, and the magnificent modern panels created by Mr R. Dunn for Gallahers and Tersons in recent years. The adaptation of traditional techniques to take advantage of improved tools and materials has enabled some of today's marquetry craftsmen to produce work which rivals the best of the past in design and execution. This book aims to introduce the pleasures of the craft to a wider public.

1

Veneers

The raw material for marquetry is the wood from many different kinds of trees, cut into thin sheets which are called veneers.

There is an erroneous impression that the use of veneer over a groundwork of other timber is necessarily a poor alternative to the use of a solid hardwood such as mahogany, rosewood and so on. This impression is perhaps strengthened by the colloquial use of the word 'veneer' to mean a superficial appearance of refinement hiding an underlying inferiority.

It is true that some cheap veneered furniture described as 'mahogany finish' or 'teak finish' may indeed be inferior and shoddy, but this apart, veneers in the hands of craftsmen have been used for centuries in order to produce beautiful furniture which could not possibly have been made from solid timber because of the great weight and density of solid hardwood, and also because of its tendency to split and warp with time. In addition, the beautiful decorative effects obtainable by matching consecutive leaves of figured veneers to give a symmetrical pattern would also be impossible with solid wood, since no two pieces could be exactly matched.

As far as marquetry is concerned, although in past centuries quite elaborate designs were executed by the inlaying of solid woods, the availability of thin veneers which can easily be cut with a knife now enables the amateur to make the most intricate designs with the simplest of tools.

In order to make marquetry pictures it is not essential to be able to recognise or identify by name the different veneers, or to know how they are cut, and from which part of the tree they come; but the more one makes use of veneers the more one comes to be fascinated by their infinite variety of colour, figuring and texture, and curious as to the origin of these features.

THE FIGURING OF VENEERS

Everyone is familiar with the appearance of a log or tree stump which has been cut across, with its pattern of concentric rings showing the annual growth of the tree; the light coloured areas representing the spring growth of wide thin walled cells, forming channels to carry the

1 *Features of a cut log*

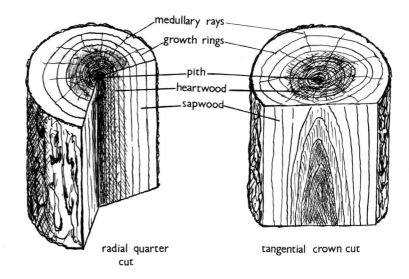

medullary rays
growth rings
pith
heartwood
sapwood

radial quarter
cut

tangential crown cut

sap to the developing leaves and flowers, and the darker areas representing the summer growth of narrow thick walled cells whose greater density gives strength to the trunk. (1)

These rings are well marked in trees grown in temperate climates where the seasons are well defined, but may be less marked or absent in tropical trees where growth continues throughout the year. It is also noticeable from the cut surface of a log that the central zone known as the *heartwood*, being the oldest part of the tree, is darker in colour than the outer zone. In this inner zone the cells have ceased to carry sap and have died, accumulating deposits of resin, tannin and gum which cause darkening and hardening of the wood compared with the living outer *sapwood* which is softer and lighter. The small area in the centre of the heartwood, the *pith*, is usually brittle and unusable, and is removed when the log is cut up into planks or veneers.

Other markings on the wood radiate outwards from the centre, crossing the growth rings at right angles; these are known as medullary

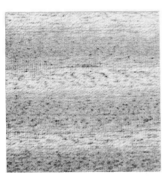

rays. A closer inspection of a piece of cut wood will also show different types of grain appearance, due to the arrangement of the wood fibres.

Straight grain is usually found in the main part of the log where the grain fibres run parallel to its length.

Irregular grain occurs where the log divides to form branches, or where there is a knot or blemish in the wood, which can be caused by an injury during growth, a disease, or insect attack.

Interlocked grain is seen in many tropical timbers, where fibres of successive growth-periods grow spirally in opposite directions, producing the familiar ribbon-striped appearance of sapele and African walnut. (2)

Wavy grain occurs when the direction of the fibres undulates. (3) The veneer surface has a shadow-striped effect at right angles to the grain direction where light is reflected in alternate ways by the wavy fibres, causing the figuring known as 'fiddle-back', often found in sycamore, maple, and African mahogany. As the name implies, this type of wood is used for making violins and other stringed musical instruments, this feature of the wood in some way contributing to the resonance of the instrument.

All these features combine to make up the distinctive figuring of the wood from a particular species of tree, but it may be seen that the exact figuring which will appear in the veneers will depend on the way in which the log is sliced up. This decision rests with the veneer cutter at the factory, and it requires considerable skill and experience to obtain the most beautifully figured veneers from any given log.

MANUFACTURE OF VENEERS

Before the logs are cut into veneers, the fibres of the wood have to be softened by steaming or boiling the logs in vats for a given time depending on the type of timber. The bark is peeled off and the logs are then cut up in one of several ways.

2 *Interlocked grain*
3 *Fiddleback figure*

4 Rotary cutting machine

5 (a) Rotary cutting
(b and c) Half rotary cutting

 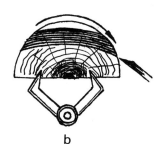 

a   b   c

Rotary cutting. The log is mounted in a machine like a huge lathe in which it rotates against a knife running the whole length of the log. This peels off a continuous sheet of veneer which is cut into convenient widths for drying and storing. Huge sheets of veneer can be obtained by this means, but with most woods the figuring would be wild and uninteresting, and this method is used mainly for the manufacture of plywood. There are however a small number of decorative veneers whose characteristic features depend on this method of cutting, and these include bird's eye maple, kevasingo and masur birch.

Half rotary cutting. The log is split lengthwise, the half or quarter log is mounted eccentrically on a stay-log and it is then cut in one of two ways as shown.

6 Flat slicing machine

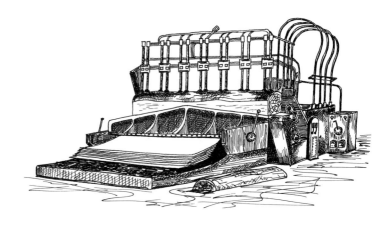

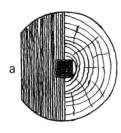

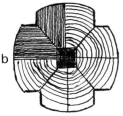

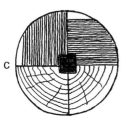

7 (a) Crown cutting
(b and c) Quarter cutting

Flat slicing. Most of the decorative veneers are obtained by slicing through the log either radially or tangentially. The log is first cut in half from end to end. The half log may then be cut into slices across its full width, producing wide veneers with a pattern of darker heartwood in the centre and lighter sapwood on either side. These veneers are known as *crown cut*, and this method is most often employed for walnut, ash, and elm veneers, which are used for panelling and cabinet making.

Alternatively the log is further divided into quarters, or into eight sections called 'flitches'. Each flitch is mounted on the slicer and cut into veneers parallel with the radius of the log. These *quarter cut* veneers are much narrower than crown cut veneers, but show up the striped figuring of woods such as sapele, African walnut, rosewood and teak. This method of cutting also brings out the distinctive medullary rays as a pronounced figuring in woods such as lacewood (plane tree) and silky oak.

Saw cutting. The use of machines with huge knife blades for veneer cutting has almost entirely superseded the old-fashioned method of cutting veneers by circular saw which produced thicker veneers with a good deal of sawdust waste. Saw cutting is now used only for a few very hard or brittle woods such as ebony; for curl veneers; and for

11

8 Veneer match from four consecutive leaves (walnut)
9 Curl veneer (rosewood)

certain woods whose colouring would be affected adversely by the preliminary steam treatment required for knife cutting.

Whichever way the veneers are cut they are always re-assembled in order before drying and storing, and the bundles of veneers are kept together to enable consecutive veneers to be matched in decorative veneering. (8)

BURRS, BUTTS AND CURLS

Apart from the veneers cut from the main part of the log, veneers with special figuring are obtained from other parts of the tree.

Curl or crotch veneers are obtained from the junction of a main branch with the trunk of a tree, and have a most attractive ostrich feather figuring. (9)

Burr veneers come from the knobbly excrescences which occur naturally on the trunks of some trees, consisting of a mass of embryonic buds.

12

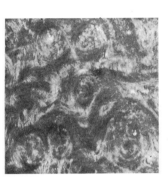

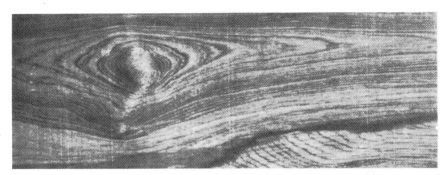

10 Burr veneer (maidu burr)
11 Unusual sheet of rose-wood, suggesting water

These veneers have a characteristic appearance of groups of small knots with highly figured surrounding grain. They tend to be porous and brittle and must be cut with great care. Pieces of burr are seldom very large. (10)

Butt veneers are of a somewhat similar appearance to curl veneers, but are obtained from the stump of the tree where the trunk spreads towards the roots.

All these fancy veneers are of limited size and are comparatively expensive because of their relative scarcity and fragility, but they are highly valued for their figuring both for marquetry and cabinet making.

In addition, occasionally freak effects are found when a log is cut up, resulting in veneers which may be useless for commercial purposes, but are of exceptional value for pictorial marquetry. An unusual grain formation, a variation from the normal colouring of the wood, sometimes even a disease or fungus affecting the wood, can result in veneers whose natural figuring may almost form a picture in itself such as a stormy sea, a stony beach, a sunset sky. (11) One cannot buy this kind of freak veneer to order, but by frequenting shops which supply a full range of veneers, and looking through their stocks, one occasionally has a 'find' of this sort which can be kept in store against the time when a suitable occasion for its use appears.

2
Types of Veneer

The number of different kinds of veneers runs into many hundreds, but of these perhaps two hundred or so are in general use, and the availability of many of these varies from time to time. It would be impossible in this book to give a detailed account of all the veneers which may be used in marquetry, so I shall give only a short description of the main groups of common veneers and a few of the less well known ones, with suggestions of possible uses for them. However, because of the natural variations occurring even in veneers of the same species cut from different logs, even a set of veneer samples, though extremely useful, cannot give a complete picture of the qualities of the veneers, much less so can a printed description. In the long run it is the appearance of an individual piece of veneer, and not its name, which determines its suitability for the purpose of the work in hand.

AMBOYNA BURR   Attractive, closely figured burr, reddish brown, rather brittle. Use for flowers or bushes in the foreground.

ANTIARIS   Light yellow colour, with interlocking grain forming shadow–stripe effect. Very soft to cut, useful as waste veneer in 'window method' cutting, or for light coloured borders.

ASH

Off-white, with the annual rings showing as alternative stripes of open grain pores and closed grain. Quarter cut veneer has straight stripes and can be used for borders. If crown cut, may have more interesting wavy figuring suitable for a sky or water.

Olive Ash   Similar to ash, but with superimposed light brown staining. When striped, is useful to indicate fences or wooden walled buildings. Irregular figuring may be used for depicting buildings partly in shadow, or to get a rounded effect for a pillar or curved wall without having recourse to sand scorching.

Japanese Ash   Straw coloured, with wild grain and attractive all-over markings. Not a veneer to use in large pieces, but effective if used with discretion.

Ash Burr   Off-white, the burr figuring often occurring in small

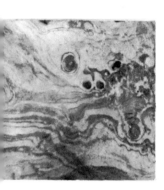

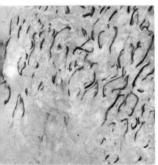

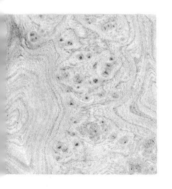

patches only; suitable for light coloured flowers or foliage.

Olive Ash Burr Colouring as for olive ash, but very wild figuring. (12)

AVODIRE Pale yellow-cream colour with oblique quilted figure, suggests cloudy sky.

BIRCH

Canadian Birch A light pinkish yellow in colour, with close grain and no distinctive figuring.

Swedish Birch Also known as ice or flame birch is lighter in colour, but with similar texture. Both are useful in portraiture, or for portraying flesh tones in any picture with human figures. May also be useful for sky, especially a cold winter sky with a suggestion of clouds.

Masur Birch Similar to Swedish birch, but contains groups of dark markings and flecks caused by a disease process affecting the tree. This veneer can be very useful for a cobbled street or pebbled beach. Sometimes the junction between a plain and figured area of the veneer can be used to indicate the hair and face of a human head with one piece of veneer, and the other features for a portrait, such as ears, may be found by careful study of the veneer. Masur birch treated as Harewood gives a good impression of lattice windows. (13)

COUBARIL A pinkish background with dark brown to black irregular striped figuring. Can give a good impression of an expanse of road or desert, giving a feeling of distance. Difficult to cut, but attractive.

ELM

Has a pinkish brown colour, fairly regularly striped when quarter cut, but with more interesting wavy figuring if crown cut.

ELM BURR Very attractive, rather porous veneer. Groups of knots in burr, useful for bushes and tree foliage, but the wild swirling figure between the knots can be used for hair, or to give the impression of a curved surface; for example, an earthenware pot or log. The most useful burr of all, in my opinion. (14)

12 *Olive ash burr*
13 *Masur birch*
14 *Elm burr*

15

GREEN CYPRESS BURR   The best green colour available in veneer, perfect for trees, bushes, and for individual leaves in flower studies. The figuring includes lighter coloured lines which can be used to indicate the veins on a leaf.

(*Caution*   Contact with acid will turn the green colour to brown. Certain polishes contain acid, and the surface of the picture must be sealed before applying the polish, or discolouration may occur.)

HAREWOOD   This is most commonly made from sycamore by chemical treatment. Its colour varies from pale silvery grey, bluish or mid-grey to dark slate colour. Figuring depends on the original wood, but may be fiddleback, stripey or plain. The lighter shades can be used to indicate shadows in a snow scene, and the darker shades for water or stone. (See also page 94.)

(*Caution*   Contact with acid causes Harewood to revert to its original colour, as above.)

HORSE CHESTNUT

The whitest veneer available, *holly* being virtually unobtainable nowadays. It has minimal figuring and grain marking. Soft and easy to cut. Can be used for white walled houses and for snow scenes. Useful also for white stringers. (See chapter on borders.) It tends to yellow gradually with exposure to light.

Horse Chestnut Burr   Very soft white burr, densely patterned with knot marks.

MACASSAR EBONY   Very hard brittle veneer, difficult to cut. Pinkish brown with black stripes. Small pieces may be used where a black colour is required. Also useful for a dark border or background.

MADRONA BURR   Medium reddish brown, quilted figure with unobtrusive knot marks.

MAGNOLIA   Light green to greenish brown colour, soft close texture with little figuring or graining, extremely easy to cut. Very useful for distant fields, grass, and for leaves in flower designs. (*Caution* as for green cypress.)

MAHOGANY

There are many different kinds, all in varying shades of reddish brown.

Honduras Mahogany Slightly lighter, and has a closer grain than *African Mahogany* which has a wavy grain with fiddleback effect.

Sapele This has a close regular stripe, often used for furniture. (See figure 2.)

Pommele A freak sapele in which the grain is broken up, giving an attractive blistered effect. (15)

Any of these woods may be used to give warmth and colour to the foreground of a picture, and may also be useful in animal and bird studies. They are also very suitable for borders.

MAKORE Reddish brown with mottled figure, useful in small pieces to add colour to a picture, especially for foreground detail. Very effective for rose petals.

MANSONIA Dark greyish brown veneer with very straight grain and no figuring. Easy to cut, useful for borders and in geometrical marquetry.

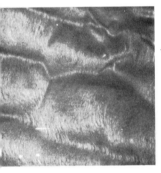

MAPLE

Pinkish straight-grained wood with few markings. Occasionally found with the grain broken up into irregular patches, and is then known as *Quilted Maple*. (16)

Figured Maple is another form. Any of these may be useful in portraiture for flesh tones. Figured and quilted maple can be used for flower studies, especially for rose petals.

Bird's Eye Maple A rotary cut veneer with many tiny circular marks scattered through the grain, the result of insect infestation which occurs naturally, but is also deliberately introduced in order to produce this veneer for commercial purposes in large quantities. (17)

Bird's Eye Greywood Bird's eye maple treated as Harewood.

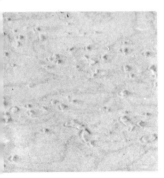

15 Pommele
16 Quilted maple
17 Bird's eye maple

Queensland Maple　A much darker wood, reddish brown in colour with a fine mottled figuring, more resembling mahogany than Canadian maple.

Maple Burr　Attractive pinkish brown, soft and easy to cut, with swirl figuring between groups of knots. Good for depicting rose petals.

MOVINGUE　A bright yellow, brittle veneer with interlocked or wavy grain. Tricky to cut, but indispensable for depicting fields of corn, haystacks, blonde hair or wherever a true yellow colour is required.

OAK

English Oak　A light beige to brown colour with distinctive grain markings and flecks formed by the medullary rays.

Brown Oak　The same wood as English Oak which has been affected by a fungus which causes rich brown streaks superimposed on the basic oak figuring. It is useful in bird and animal pictures, and for thatch, fences and walls.

Australian Silky Oak　Pinkish brown with a well marked fleck which may be small and regular to give a basketwork effect, or quite large and irregularly placed, useful to depict a wall or bridge of stones. Despite its name it is a different species of tree from the English oak, and the veneer is more like lacewood.

Oak Burr　Dull light brown with groups of small darker knots.

OBECHE　Plain obeche is a soft, very open grained, straw coloured veneer, which can be used as a 'waste veneer'. Occasionally the log is affected by a fungus which causes a streaky blue colouring known as *Blue stained Obeche*, making an ideal veneer for a summer sky, or if the staining is very dark and pronounced, it can be used for sea or lake water.

PADAUK *(Andaman)*　A brilliant scarlet red colour. Rather brittle and open grained with little figuring. Needs to be used with discretion and in small pieces, but is very effective to add colour, for jackets in hunting scenes, lips in portraits, etc. (*Caution*　The colour of this veneer tends to run into adjacent veneers when moisture, e.g. glue,

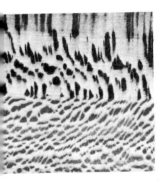

sealer or polish, is applied. This may be avoided by giving both sides of the veneer sheet two or three coats of sanding sealer before starting to cut pieces out of it.)

PLANETREE (LACEWOOD)

Pinkish to orange-brown colour with a lacelike figure of small darker flecks formed by the medullary rays. According to the way in which the veneer is cut, these may give a uniform basket weave figure where the rays are cut across, or elongated lines at right angles to the grain direction where the quarter cut veneer cuts the medullary rays lengthways. (18)

Grey Lacewood   Planetree treated chemically as Harewood. Useful for depicting stonework.

Planetree Burr   Groups of very small dark flecks in undulating background. An attractive veneer, could be used to show hair on a human or animal figure.

PURPLEHEART   As the name suggests, a purple-violet colour. Straight grained with little figuring. Best used in small pieces.

ROSA PEROBA   Very attractive and unusual salmon pink colour, sometimes with darker pink stripes. Occasionally found with freak figuring which may give a good sunset sky effect.

ROSEWOOD

There are several types of rosewood, all of which are brittle and very difficult to cut, but they polish well and are attractive enough to be worth the trouble of cutting.

Rio or Brazilian Rosewood   A reddish brown with black markings; may be striped, often almost black in places, elsewhere may have attractive wild figuring suggestive of rough water or a night sky. If straight grained it can make a good border.

Bombay or Indian Rosewood   This has purplish stripes on brown background.

Madagascar Rosewood   Much lighter in colour, reddish brown markings on light brown background. Pronounced flecks from medullary rays not unlike lacewood.

SYCAMORE

White wood, may be plain, faintly striped or figured, often with fiddleback markings. *Figured sycamore* may be useful for sky or water.

Weathered Sycamore   Pinkish yellow with similar markings.

TEAK   Brownish, fairly straight grained with darker stripes. Good for borders and in pictures for fences, boats, thatch, and to depict anything wooden.

THUYA BURR   Mid-brown burr with groups of very small, almost black knot marks.

VAVONA BURR   Rich dark reddish brown burr with typical burr figuring.

WALNUT

Innumerable kinds of walnut come from different countries, varying in colour from light pinkish brown to almost black. It is easy to cut.

English Walnut   Mid-brown with deeper brown figuring.

American Walnut   Darker brown with deeper greyish-black markings.

French Charbonnier Walnut   Very dark in places, may have areas of true black, useful for marquetry as it is the only really black veneer which is easy to cut.

Nigerian or African Walnut   This is not a true member of the walnut family, and more closely resembles sapele in texture, having the same shadow-striped appearance but in a golden brown colour. Useful for borders.

Walnut Burr   This also varies in colour from light to very dark brown, very useful for depicting bushes or trees.

20

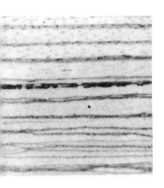

9 Zebrano

The great variety of colour and figuring obtainable makes walnut among the most useful veneers for marquetry.

WENGE   A dark brown wood with very fine, close black stripes. Effective where a really dark border is desired, and also to show the beams of timbered houses or other dark wooden structures.

ZEBRANO   Stripes of brown on buff coloured background. Coarse open grain. The width of the stripes varies. May be used to suggest tiled roofs or wooden clad building or fence. (19)

ROSE ZEBRANO   Similarly striped veneer with pink background.

As already mentioned, this is by no means a comprehensive list of the available veneers, but may serve to give an indication of the wide range of colours and types of figuring which can be found. Over a period of years most marquetarians accumulate a stock of veneers of many kinds, and occasional visits to a veneer merchant will usually add a few more interesting pieces to the collection for only a small outlay of money.

3
Tools and Equipment

20 Tools for marquetry

Marquetarians acquire in time a large assortment of tools and gadgets for their craft, but the basic essentials are few and inexpensive. The main requirements are: a knife, sharpening stone, cutting board, carbon and tracing paper, gummed tape and glue.

KNIVES

The knife is by far the most important item of equipment, and it is worth taking a little trouble to find one which you find comfortable to hold, and which is easy to use. Almost all the cutting is done with the point of the blade, so the most useful shape is one which tapers to a fine point. The blade itself should be thin, but not too fragile.

A penknife, or other knife with a fixed blade is usually found to be too thick to make a clean cut, but there are a number of craft tools on the market now which consist of a handle with several thin blades of different shapes and sizes which are interchangeable, and replacement blades can be obtained quite cheaply. An alternative is to get a surgical

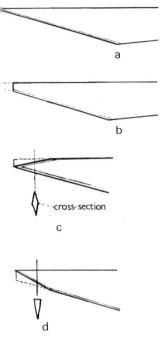

scalpel handle for which packets of blades are available in different sizes. These are a little finer than those in most craft knives, but though they are more fragile, they are very sharp and cut the veneer easily. The handle, being flat, is comfortable to hold.

There are two useful sizes of scalpel handle, Nos 3 & 4, each with several shapes of blades to fit. I use the No. 4 handle with a size 23 blade, which has a curved edge, for heavy cutting, e.g. when cutting borders against a straight edge; but I prefer the No. 3 handle with a size 11 blade for almost all other cutting, especially for the fine details of a picture. This blade has a straight cutting edge, and tapers to a very fine point.

Marquetarians by trial and error find knives to suit themselves from the great variety available. Some recommend a knife made from a piece of hacksaw blade, broken off at an angle of 30°, and then ground down, sharpened on an oilstone and fitted into a handle. One man who has won awards for his excellent marquetry pictures does all his cutting with pieces of razor blades broken into pointed fragments, and held in his fingers—a method not to be generally recommended. In fact, the knives which are available commercially are so cheap and easily obtained, that it is advisable to buy one.

SHARPENING THE KNIFE

The knife once chosen, it is essential to keep it sharp. If the knife is blunt the cutting of the veneer becomes very hard work, and may result in split veneers, broken knife blades, cut fingers and bad temper. A few strokes of the blade on a small oilstone every ten to fifteen minutes whilst cutting is usually sufficient, though when cutting very hard or brittle veneers the knife may need to be sharpened more often.

When the point of the blade breaks it is best to form a new point by sharpening from the top (blunt) edge of the blade, to maintain its tapered shape, and to give the point two cutting edges (21 a, b, c). A blade tip kept sharpened in this way from both edges has a diamond-shaped cross section which gives a narrow cut, and slides easily through the veneer because of its streamlined shape. (If the blade is sharpened from one edge only, its cross section remains triangular, making

21 Sharpening knife blade

cutting more difficult, and causing the blade to break sooner.) (21d)

CUTTING BOARD

The cutting board should be of fairly soft wood so that the knife point is not blunted when it sinks into the board after cutting through the veneers. Hardboard can be used, but this quickly tends to become furrowed, and the knife point may get caught, resulting in a false cut. Plywood is preferable, about $\frac{3}{8}$ in. to $\frac{1}{2}$ in. thickness, and of any convenient size, such as 14 in. $\times$ 12 in.

If the picture you are making is of a suitable size, it is quite a good idea to use the baseboard, on which you later intend to mount the picture, as a cutting board during the early stages. The series of cuts and scratches which appear on its surface provide a 'key' for the glue when you mount the picture and backing, so both sides of the board should be used.

CARBON PAPER

Thin black carbon paper should be used for transferring the design on to the veneer with a fine pointed stylo. This leaves only a narrow line which virtually disappears as the knife cuts along it. (Blue carbon paper leaves indelible blue lines on the veneer, and when any glue or moisture touches it the blue dye can penetrate deeply into the wood, and is then impossible to remove.) Yellow carbon paper is also available which is useful for tracing on to the darker veneers.

The stylo I use is made from an old fine steel crochet hook, with the hook broken off, and the shank filed down to a smooth point. Alternatively a spent ball point pen may be used for tracing, but this makes a wider line.

GUMMED PAPER

For holding together the parts of the picture as they are assembled, thin gummed brown paper tape is ideal as it can be removed easily afterwards simply by damping the paper. It is available in rolls one inch in width. It is best to avoid using *Sellotape* for this purpose as it adheres so strongly that when it is removed, some of the fibres from the coarse-grained veneers may be lifted off with the tape, and some of the adhesive tends to get lodged in the pores of the veneer. There are however one or two occasions when *Sellotape* can be useful, so a roll of this should also be at hand.

GLUE

A quick setting glue is used instead of tape for holding the smaller pieces of the picture together. Balsa cement is suitable for this purpose, or a PVA white glue, which dries transparent, or a clear glue such as Uhu, Bostik, Evostik Clear or Elmer's Glue-All. A different type of glue is required for laying the completed picture, and this will be discussed in a later chapter.

4

Designs for Marquetry

Most people who take up marquetry make their first pictures from bought Marquetry kits. These have a design with veneers numbered to correspond with the parts of the picture for which each is to be used. With all the materials to hand in this way, it is possible to concentrate entirely on the purely mechanical matter of cutting the picture. Once the basic principles of cutting and assembling the picture have been mastered however, the marquetarian begins to look for an opportunity to exercise his skill and ingenuity in choosing a design for himself, and in making his own selection of veneers in order to complete a picture which he can really regard as his own creation. One must consider therefore the possible sources of designs which may be adapted to make them suitable for execution in marquetry.

Unfortunately, few marquetarians are also artists in their own right, and most find it necessary to obtain designs from other sources. Personally I cannot see any real harm in this. I think it is better to use a good design drawn by somebody else than to waste hours of work cutting a picture from a home-made drawing which, though original, may at best be lacking in artistic merit, and at worst may be full of elementary errors in composition and perspective. Historically, the marquetry craftsmen of the past had their designs provided for them by artists, but nowadays few are so fortunate as to have an artist on hand to supply a design when required. Consequently most people look for a design which appeals to them, perhaps from a book illustration, calendar, magazine advertisement, photograph, Christmas card or similar source, and adapt it as necessary to make it suitable for reproduction in marquetry. The amount of simplification necessary will obviously depend to some extent on the marquetry skill of the person who is to make up the picture—the beginner would be well advised to look for bold simple outlines, and rely on well chosen veneers to add interest and texture, whereas the more advanced craftsman can put in more intricate outlines and finer details to enhance the effect.

Figures 22 a and b show a marquetry picture, and the picture on which it is based—originally an oil painting, but reproduced on a birthday card. This shows quite well the sort of adaptation which is necessary—the branches on the trees are simplified, the folds of the

*22 Adaptation of a picture
for marquetry*
a Country Friends *Eric
Tansley*
b Nature's Compensations
*12 in. × 14 in. marquetry
picture by C. H. Good*

tramps's clothes are cut in in some detail, but the features of the log are effectively represented by a single piece of figured veneer.

It is often better to start with a black and white picture than with a coloured one. Working from a coloured original there is a tendency to try to match the colours exactly with the veneers, which soon becomes an impossible feat; whereas with a black and white design one is more likely to concentrate on tonal values—indicated in the design by shading—and to achieve the correct effect by the depth of tone in the veneers selected, rather than entirely by colour. For this reason I find that wood engravings in particular seem to lend themselves to being used for marquetry designs.

The use of such original works of art may be open to criticism on the grounds that the result of translation to one artistic medium of a design conceived for a different medium is seldom as effective as the

27

original version, rather like a tapestry copy of the *Laughing Cavalier*. Certainly, I should not myself care to embark on a marquetry version of that picture, though no doubt this has been done. In fact I have seen one or two strikingly successful marquetry pictures based on famous paintings but these are definitely exceptions. The version of *Pinkie* (23b), is in my opinion, one of these. Perhaps the answer is that if you are using someone else's talent, it is better not to start with an acknowledged masterpiece, but with the sort of design in which the use of veneer can give an additional interest, rather than a poor imitation.

It must be clear from the foregoing that most marquetry pictures, including those illustrating this book, take their origin from various sources which it is often impossible to trace or to acknowledge. In the same way as they collect veneers, people tend to pick up odd pictures and designs here and there for possible use in the future, and can seldom remember exactly where each came from.

Where the main requirement for a design is an accurate representation of something from nature—animal, bird or flower—there is less of a problem. Illustrations from books on these subjects can make very attractive marquetry pictures, while an original floral composition can be made up with the aid of a nurseryman's catalogue.

Alternatively, floral motifs and other suitable designs may be found in embroidery patterns, which include line drawings already prepared, and usually coloured representation of the finished design. The miniature *Cotswold Village* (see figure 23a) originated from an embroidery design. The design was actually for a firescreen, but I used the small photograph of the finished firescreen which was included with the embroidery pattern, and reproduced that in marquetry in actual size, i.e. $2\frac{1}{2}$ in. $\times$ 3 in.

DESIGNS FROM PHOTOGRAPHS

Photographs are a useful source of designs, and if you take the photograph yourself there can be no problem about copyright or accusation of plagiarism. A black and white photograph can be converted directly into a line drawing fairly easily, and this avoids the difficulties of trying to make out the outlines through tracing paper.

28

23a Cotswold Village
M. R. Campkin

23b Pinkie
Mrs G. M. Walker

Method Obtain two prints of the photograph, preferably enlarged to the exact size of the proposed picture, as this saves the trouble of scaling the picture up or down. The prints should be on matt surfaced bromide paper. Keep one photograph for reference when making up the picture later.

On the second print, using waterproof Indian ink and a fine pen, go over the outlines of the photograph, including all the features which are to appear in the line drawing, but omitting any unwanted details. If any difficulty is experienced in getting the ink to 'take' it can be remedied by dusting the surface of the photograph lightly with french chalk.

When the outlines of the picture are completed, the finer details can be added, shadows, and shading. The second print will help in checking these. When all the desired features have been inked in, the photograph must be allowed to dry thoroughly.

There are now two ways of bleaching out the photograph.

1   Make up a solution of iodine, using a 5 per cent solution of potassium iodide in water, and then adding as many iodine crystals as will dissolve in it.

Lay the photograph in a flat dish in this solution until the photographic image has disappeared, leaving only a brown stain. Rinse in cold water, then transfer to a bath of photographer's hypo (1 oz in 5 oz water) until the stain has cleared. Rinse well for two or three minutes in running water, then hang up to dry.

2   For the other method, a solution of hypo is made as above (1 part hypo to 5 of water). Just before the bath is required add a 10 per cent solution of potassium ferricyanide (1 oz to 10 oz water) using sufficient to make the solution straw-coloured. (Alternatively, to 1 oz of diluted hypo add 20 grains of potassium ferricyanide.) This solution must not be made up until it is required. Immediately place the photograph in the solution and leave until the image has completely disappeared leaving only the inked lines. Wash in running water until all the yellow stains have disappeared then leave to dry. Be careful not to touch the surface of the print whilst it is wet as it is easily damaged.

You will now have a line drawing with clear simple outlines to work from, while keeping the original photograph to refer to when deciding on the veneers to be used to give the correct tone variations for the picture.

Many people now take coloured transparencies, and it may be that you would like to use one of these for a design. One method of doing this is to use a slide projector. Pin a sheet of white paper to the wall, and set up the projector so that the image falls on to the paper. (The drawing can be made to any size by adjusting the distance between the projector and the paper.) Then draw the outlines of the picture on to the paper. One disadvantage is that the hand holding the pencil may obliterate part of the picture. This could be overcome by using a sheet of frosted glass fixed upright a suitable distance from the projector, with a sheet of tracing paper taped to the opposite side, and draw the picture from this side. In the latter case the slide should be put into the projector back to front, as the image will be in reverse.

A great variety of compositions can now be made using a little ingenuity. For example, if a photograph features a street scene with a horse and cart in the middle distance, and you wish to make them more prominent, first trace the details of the background on to the paper, omitting the horse and cart, then move the projector a little further away to make them bigger, and draw them on to the picture. In the same way a picture could be built up using features from different transparencies to obtain the desired composition.

It is possible to have black and white photographs made into slides which can be projected in the same way; or if you have an epidiascope the same method could be used as a means of adapting or enlarging any photograph or picture. This could be useful, for example, if a picture were being taken from a book, where tracing would damage the page. As a means of enlarging a picture to any scale it is considerably quicker than the usual method of using squared paper.

DESIGN FROM THE VENEER ITSELF

Perhaps the most truly artistic form of marquetry is that in which instead of the veneers being selected to fit the design, the design itself is dictated by the naturally occurring features of one or more pieces of veneer. In such a picture, the main part of the picture might consist of only one or two large pieces of veneer having within their figuring

23c Evening on the Nile
E. W. G. Hawkins

all the features, for example, of a stormy sea and a wild sky. Into this background may be inserted some focus of interest such as a group of boats, or some foreground figures or buildings to complement the natural beauty of the background veneers (see also figure 23c). In my opinion marquetry comes to be an art form in its own right when the unique qualities of the natural wood veneers are exploited in this way.

5

Cutting a Picture

After obtaining a suitable design, the next step is to begin building up the design in veneers. There are several ways of doing this.

'STICK AS YOU GO' METHOD

Commercial kits often have the design printed on the baseboard, with instructions to trace each piece of the design in turn on to the appropriate veneer with carbon paper, cut round the outline, and stick the piece in place on the baseboard. Unfortunately one soon discovers that no matter how carefully the tracing and cutting are done, the adjacent pieces seldom seem to fit exactly together. It is almost impossible to trace the same line twice without deviating a little in places, and even this small amount leaves an unsightly gap in the finished picture.

POUNCING METHOD

One method of making sure that the outline is exactly reproduced is by 'pouncing', i.e. by pricking a series of fine holes along all the lines of the design with a needle. The various parts of the picture are transferred to separate pieces of paper by dabbing through the pricked design with bitumen powder on a felt dabber, or in a fine muslin bag. The powder is fixed to the underlying paper by gentle heating, giving a fine dotted outline which can be repeatedly reproduced without any variation. Each of these pieces of paper is then glued to the appropriate veneer and the piece is cut out and stuck in place. (See figures 35a, b.)

Even so, in cutting out the piece of veneer it is not always possible to keep absolutely to the line without the slightest deviation of the knife and the pieces may still not fit well together. In addition, pricking out the picture is rather a slow and tedious process, but this method may have its uses in some kinds of fretsaw cutting as we shall see later. (Pricking the design could be done more quickly using an unthreaded sewing machine to prick the main outlines, then finishing the intricate details by hand.)

TEMPLATE METHOD

A considerable step towards overcoming the difficulties of accurate cutting is to use one piece of the picture when cut as a guide or template

*24 Design for a marquetry
picture*

Suggested veneers for design *(Arrows indicate grain direction)*

1	Dark walnut burr	7	Medium walnut
2	Light walnut burr or oak burr	8	Horse chestnut or sycamore
3	Green cypress burr	9	Weathered sycamore
4	Rosewood	10	Plane tree (Lacewood)
5	Grey lacewood or harewood	11	Olive ash
	(a) dark, (b) light	12	Magnolia (a) dark, (b) light
6	Light walnut	13	Birch, avodire or obeche

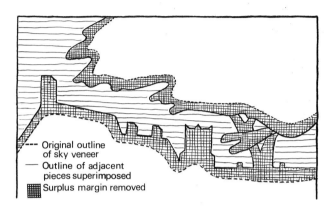

for cutting the adjacent part of the next piece of the picture. For example, in the design in figure 24, the outline of the sky is traced on to the appropriate veneer using carbon paper, including details of roof, chimneys and tree trunk. The sky veneer is then cut out leaving a small surplus margin all round (about $\frac{1}{4}$ in.) except for the outer border which can be cut accurately with a ruler. This piece is glued in place on the baseboard.

For the moment considering the tree veneer to be all in one piece, this outline would next be traced on to the chosen veneer and cut exactly to size all round. This piece is then fixed in place with a single dab of balsa cement or glue (or with two or three small pieces of *Sellotape*) on to the baseboard, overlapping the surplus sky veneer.

The sky veneer can now be cut to exact shape along this outline, keeping the knife pressed against the edge of the tree veneer for an accurate cut. When the whole outline has been cut through, the tree veneer is lifted off, before the glue has had time to set firmly (or by removing the *Sellotape*). The surplus margin of the sky veneer is now prised up, and the tree veneer glued firmly in place, this time covering the whole under surface with glue. The next step is to put in the large left hand roof, cutting it exactly to size along the upper edge where it adjoins the sky veneer, but leaving a surplus at the sides and lower edge. Then the other roofs, the church tower—ignoring details of windows, chimneys and spires for the present—then the walls, and so on, working downwards.

35

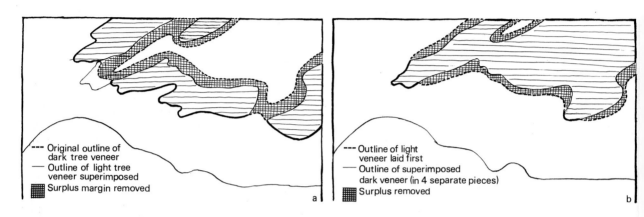

--- Original outline of
dark tree veneer
— Outline of light tree
veneer superimposed
▓ Surplus margin removed

a

--- Outline of light
veneer laid first
— Outline of superimposed
dark veneer (in 4 separate pieces)
▓ Surplus removed

b

26a and b Two ways of
cutting tree veneers

The tree trunk is only put in after all the necessary underlying background is in place, and the small details last of all. These are done by superimposing, for example, a chimney cut to size on the sky in the appropriate place, cutting round the outline, removing the underlying veneer and gluing the piece into position.

(Returning to the subject of the tree veneer, if this is to be put in as in the original design, two methods are possible, as shown in the diagrams.) The first is quicker, involving the cutting and insertion of two pieces only, first the darker outer part of the tree in one piece, and then the lighter part. The second allows more versatility in choosing differently figured pieces of the darker veneer by inserting each piece separately after first laying the lighter veneer.)

THE 'WINDOW' METHOD

This is a development of the template method, but has some additional advantages. Basically it consists of tracing the whole picture on to a spare sheet of veneer, cutting out each piece of the picture in turn, and replacing it with the chosen veneer using the hole or 'window' in the waste veneer as a template to get an accurate fit. In this way the picture is gradually built up in veneer form, and only after all cutting has been completed is it finally glued on to the baseboard. This enables alterations to be made at any stage, should a piece of veneer fit badly, or look unsuitable. The other advantage is that as each 'window' is cut, the

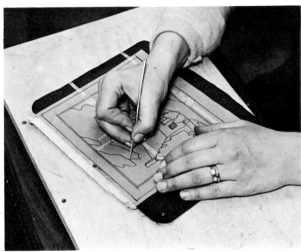

27-28

effect of different veneers can be tried in the context of the rest of the picture, until exactly the desired effect is obtained.

The procedure is as follows:

The waste veneer should be light in colour, easy to cut, and at least an inch larger all round than the picture is to be. Obeche, sycamore or horse chestnut are all suitable. (It is often possible to use the veneer which will represent the sky as the waste veneer if a large enough piece is available. In effect this means that the first piece is already in position. Similarly in a design consisting for example of a spray of flowers against a background, the background veneer would take the place of the waste veneer.) The edges of the waste veneer are reinforced with gummed paper tape to prevent splitting.

The line drawing is transferred to tracing paper, and this is hinged to the top of the waste veneer with gummed tape so that it can be lifted and replaced exactly in position (27). The main features of the picture, including the borders, are traced on to the waste veneer using black carbon paper and a fine stylo to give as fine a line as possible (28). The tracing is turned back and the first piece is cut out—either the sky, or, if the veneer already represents the sky, as in this example, the tree would be the first piece (29). The line should be followed as exactly as possible, using the point of the knife to make a series of short pricking

29–30

cuts rather than a long sweep. Where the line is very intricate the pricks should be very small and close together. No attempt should be made to cut right through the veneer at once—it may be necessary to go over the line several times before the piece is free. When the piece being cut out includes the border, this should be cut about $\frac{1}{4}$ in. oversize to allow for trimming later.

When the piece has been removed, a hole or 'window' is left in the waste veneer. Various suitable veneers can be placed behind the window and turned about until the best effect is obtained. The chosen veneer is then fixed in position with one or two pieces of Sellotape to the back of the waste veneer and the outline is marked with the point of the knife, using the edge of the 'window' as a guide (30). When this scoring cut has been made, the tree veneer can be detached and removed to the cutting board, and the cut completed. The cut piece is then fitted into place, and held with a few pieces of gummed paper tape (31). About $\frac{1}{4}$ in. $\times$ $\frac{1}{2}$ in. pieces are quite big enough, otherwise too many layers of tape will accumulate on the back making cutting difficult. The cut piece should fit closely, and if accurately cut will only fit if pressed in from the back.

The next piece of the picture is cut in the same way, again leaving a 'window', a suitable veneer is chosen, fixed with tape, and the next

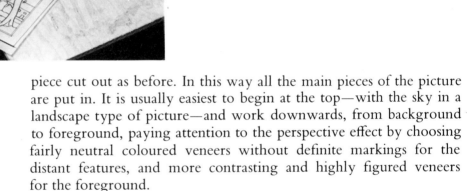

piece cut out as before. In this way all the main pieces of the picture are put in. It is usually easiest to begin at the top—with the sky in a landscape type of picture—and work downwards, from background to foreground, paying attention to the perspective effect by choosing fairly neutral coloured veneers without definite markings for the distant features, and more contrasting and highly figured veneers for the foreground.

At this stage the picture will probably consist of about six or eight main pieces, sky, hills, fields, and so on, and most or all of the original waste veneer will have disappeared. The tracing and carbon paper are now replaced, the borders are redrawn (having disappeared as the edge pieces were cut oversize) and the main details of the picture are traced in.

These smaller features of the picture are now cut in as before. These might be such items as buildings, trees, bushes and hedges. When cutting these smaller pieces, instead of taping the piece into place, it is often easier to 'butt-joint' it; that is, to spread a little quick drying glue—balsa, PVA or clear glue—on the edges of the piece of veneer, and press it into place where it will hold perfectly well. This avoids the build up of too many layers of tape on the back which later have to be removed.

Finally, the smallest details of all are traced on to the picture, such as windows and doors on buildings, individual flowers or stones in the foreground, and so on, and cut out in the same way.

The diagrams show successive stages in building up the given design.

32a, b, c, d Stages in building up the picture

You will now have the complete picture in veneer form, still capable of alteration if necessary. If it is held up to the light you will soon see if there are any really bad joins. There should only be a hairline of daylight visible between the pieces, so if one or two pieces are badly fitting, now is the time to replace them. Take a look at the picture from a distance; any badly chosen veneers which spoil the perspective effect should then be apparent; again it is better to replace them at this stage than to be irritated by them forever once the picture has been finished.

To get the true effect of the veneers as they will appear when polished, the face of the picture can be wiped over with a rag moistened with methylated spirit, or preferably sanding sealer. Some veneers, particularly the darker ones, change quite a lot, becoming darker and the figuring more prominent. For this reason, when testing the various veneers behind the 'window', it may be advisable to try the effect of moistening the surface slightly to make sure that you know how the veneer will appear in the finished picture.

If the perspective and general appearance of the picture are still satisfactory after applying this test, the picture can be put on one side for a while, preferably flat and under a weight to prevent buckling, while attention is turned to preparing the baseboard and borders.

HINTS ON CUTTING

1   Always have a good light shining directly downwards on the work to avoid shadows. An anglepoise lamp is ideal.

2   Once some experience in cutting has been obtained it is usually possible to omit taping the veneer in place before cutting: the two veneers can be held together by finger pressure. The actual cutting is best done by resting the wrist firmly on the cutting board, keeping the knife in one position with the cutting edge of the blade pointing towards you and moving the veneers with the other hand as you cut along the line, rather than by trying to turn the knife in different directions to follow the outline. This method gives more control over the knife, and avoids slips and false cuts.

3   When cutting first the 'window' and then the fitting piece it is a

33 Cutting completed

41

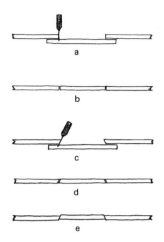

34 Straight and bevel cutting

good idea to angle the knife *very slightly* so that there is a slight bevel on the pieces. It can be seen from the diagrams why pieces cut in this way will only fit from the back, and how close a fit is achieved. The slight variations in level between the veneers are corrected later when the picture is laid and sanded.

4   Where the piece being cut has a sharp point or angle, always cut from the apex towards the base, otherwise the point will break off.

5   If a veneer is brittle and tends to split when cut, before trying to cut an intricate outline strengthen the veneer by rubbing in a little glue, front and back, and allowing it to dry. As a last resort, a piece of *Sellotape* may be stuck on the front surface to hold it together while cutting, though this may be difficult to remove afterwards.

6   The harder and more brittle the veneer to be cut, the more important it is to keep the knife sharp, and more frequent sharpening will be required. When cutting very hard veneers such as ebony and rosewood, a useful aid is an old piece of wax candle into which the point of the knife is stuck from time to time. This seems to have the effect of lubricating the blade, and makes cutting easier, and broken blades less frequent.

7   Avoid using a ruler or straight-edge when cutting a picture. Walls, fences, windows and other straight lines should be cut by hand; the slight deviations from the exact line look natural, whereas ruled lines are too regular and can spoil the appearance of the picture.

8   If a veneer to be used is buckled or warped it should be dampened slightly and put between layers of blotting paper in a press, or under a weight overnight. When dry it will be quite flat.

6
Fretsaw Cutting

This is the original method of marquetry cutting, dating from the time when the veneers available were too thick to be cut with a knife. Nowadays a form of fretsaw cutting, using the powered swing saw, is still used for the commercial production of marquetry for the furniture trade, since by this means it is possible to cut quite a large number of pieces simultaneously instead of one by one, and so to produce many identical designs at once.

The 'marquetry cutter's donkey' of former days is still used by a few professional marquetry craftsmen for the cutting of individual panels, and in the restoration of old marquetry furniture. This machine consists of a seat astride which the worker sits, with a foot treadle to operate a pair of vertical jaws, which hold and release the piece of work being sawn while the worker adjusts its position with his left hand. Meanwhile the fine saw blade, which is mounted horizontally in a frame, and moves backwards and forwards in one position, is operated by the other hand.

The wood being cut may consist of a pad of identical veneers covered by a paper pattern showing the cutting lines, or, where only one piece is to be cut, the chosen veneer sandwiched between two other veneers with the pattern on top.

Fretsaw cutting by the amateur at home follows the same principle, except that usually the work is placed horizontally on a fretsaw cutting table, and the saw is held with the blade vertical.

POUNCING METHOD

The method of reproducing the design by pouncing was described in the previous chapter. A separate paper pattern is made in this way for each piece of the design. (35a, b)

An alternative method is to obtain several copies of the design by some form of duplication, blueprint, photostat, etc., and cut these up to make the patterns. Each paper pattern must contain the whole outline of the piece to be cut—hence the need for several copies. The paper itself is *not* cut along the outline.

Single pieces of the design may then be cut by gluing the pattern on to the appropriate veneer, and taping a waste veneer underneath to

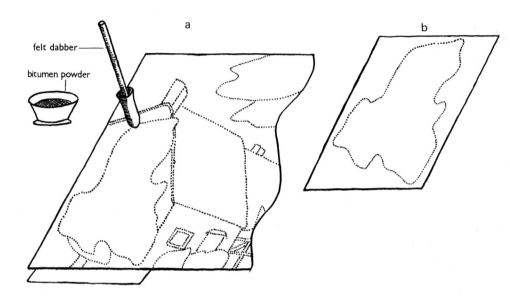

35a and b Pouncing

felt dabber

bitumen powder

a

b

take the saw-rag. The finest fretsaw blade is used, and with the blade upright and cutting exactly to the line each piece is cut out in turn. Where there is an 'island' piece, for example a window in a house, a hole must be made in the waste—in this case the window space—and the saw threaded through the hole to cut the piece out.

As the pieces are cut out they may either be glued down on to a baseboard printed with the design, or, preferably, assembled on a spare copy of the design and taped together, to be laid as a single sheet when cutting is complete.

MULTIPLE CUTTING

This method may be used when it is desired to make several copies of a design simultaneously. For each piece of the design the required number of pieces of the chosen veneer are assembled with the grain direction running the same way in each. The pieces are made into a pad with at least $\frac{1}{2}$ in. overlap all round the outline to be cut. The pattern with the outline is glued on top and a waste veneer is placed underneath, and the whole is held together by stapling or nailing with veneer pins

44

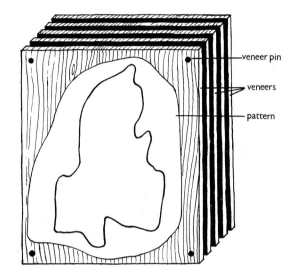

through the waste margin. The protruding heads or points of the veneer pins are nipped off before cutting starts. It is essential when cutting to keep the saw blade exactly vertical so that all the pieces will be identical in shape and size.

This method may be used if marquetry is being done for profit, but pictures made in this way will not compare with those in which each piece has been individually chosen and cut out. It could, however, be useful where several identical motifs are required, for example in making a set of table mats.

PAD METHOD

In this method all the veneers for the different parts of the picture are cut oversize and arranged together in layers, with each veneer in its appropriate position relative to the design. The sandwich of veneers so made is stapled together with a spare veneer underneath and the design on top, and the whole design is cut out in a single operation. This method has limited application, but for those interested, a detailed description may be found in *Marquetry and Veneers* by E. Kitson, or in

45

The Veneer Craftsman's Manual by W. Lincoln. It is used more in America, where the veneers available are often too thick to be cut with a knife and fretsaw techniques predominate, when this particular method may provide a suitable introduction for the beginner to the craft.

THE PIERCING BLADE METHOD

This is the most advanced form of fretsaw cutting and the only one to give results comparable with those obtained by knife cutting by the 'window method'. It is particularly useful where an intricate line has to be cut using very hard, brittle or difficult veneers.

THE BLADES

An ordinary fretsaw frame is used, but the blades are much finer than the finest fretsaw blades—Piercing Blades look no thicker than a piece of thread, and the different grades have from 40 to 80 teeth to the inch. Despite their apparent fragility these blades are used by jewellers for cutting metal, so they will go through the toughest veneer without difficulty. The blade will of course snap if the cutting is not done smoothly, but as they only cost a few pence each one's initial efforts need not be too costly. The first experiments should be made with the coarser blades—grade 1 and 2/0, graduating to 4/0 and 6/0 as experience is gained.

THE CUTTING TABLE

For the fretsaw methods previously described an ordinary flat fretsaw cutting table is used, as the work must be kept flat and the saw vertical to make a perpendicular cut. The cutting table may be a bought one, or can be improvised by cutting a narrow V-shaped slot in a plywood cutting board, and using clamps to secure it to the workbench.

With the piercing blade method however, as in the window method, the best results depend on the use of a bevel cut, for the reasons already explained. To achieve this without having to hold the saw at an angle,

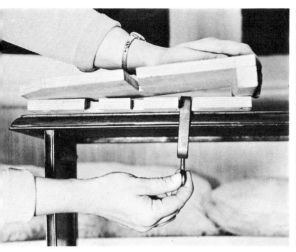

7 Clamping the angled
cutting table
8 Tools for the piercing
blade method

the cutting table is tilted at 10–15° from the horizontal. In cutting, the blade is kept vertical as before, so with the work supported at an angle a uniform bevel cut is obtained all the time.

Two further gadgets are required, a fine pointed awl, or a darning needle mounted in a handle, and a knife with a thin flat blade—an old kitchen knife is quite suitable.

A quick-drying glue such as balsa cement is used.

PROCEDURE

Basically similar to the window method, this method also starts with the design traced on to a waste veneer which will be replaced piece by piece by the veneers for the picture. However, instead of first cutting the 'window' and then the chosen veneer, in this case the chosen veneer is fixed in place behind the waste veneer and the two are cut simultaneously along the outline, so that a perfect fit is guaranteed. Where it is desired to use the 'window' procedure to aid in the selection of veneer and grain direction, a small window may be cut in the waste veneer with a knife, keeping at least $\frac{1}{4}$ in. inside the actual design line. Here, the roof of the large house is being cut, and a small window has been made to choose the veneer.

47

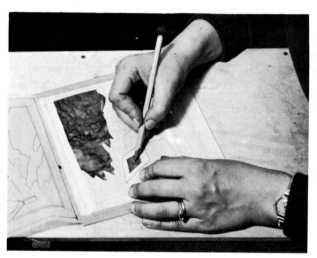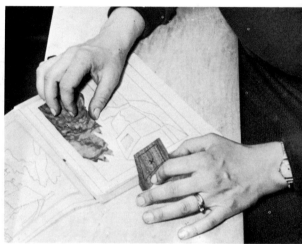

39-40

When the chosen veneer is correctly positioned behind this 'window' a locating mark can be made on it in pencil (39). It is then removed and placed under the tracing; the piece to be cut is traced on it, and the veneer is cut out roughly with a knife to leave at least $\frac{1}{4}$ in. margin round the traced outline (40). (With experience these steps can be omitted, and the veneer can be chosen and cut to size by eye.) The veneer patch so obtained is now glued into position on the underside of the waste veneer, by spreading a little balsa cement round where the cutting line will be, and is then left under a weight for a few minutes until the cement has set just firmly enough to resist the pull of the saw. If it is left too long there may be difficulty in separating the pieces after cutting.

The awl or needle is used to make a tiny hole through the two veneers, on the line to be cut (41), and through this hole the saw blade is to be introduced. If this hole is made vertically while the veneers lie on the angled cutting table, it will be at the correct angle for the saw to commence cutting (42).

As the pieces are to be let in from the back, the bevel cut must be outwards so that the underneath veneer will be slightly oversize for a good fit. It will be found that with the slope of the cutting table upwards to the right, the saw cut must be made in a clockwise direction

41

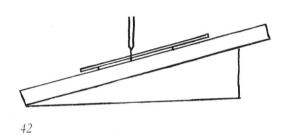

42

43 *Method of cutting with
veneer patch underneath*

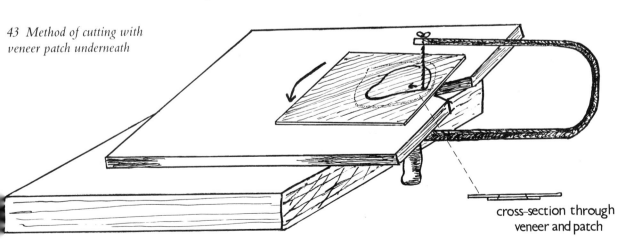

cross-section through
veneer and patch

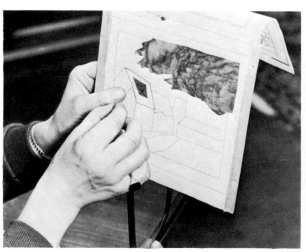
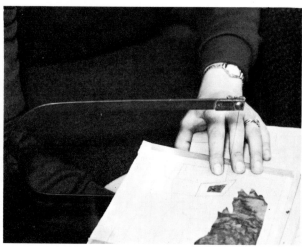

44-45

round the outline, i.e. the veneer is turned anti-clockwise towards the saw as cutting proceeds. (43)

The blade is fixed in the lower part of the fretsaw frame with the teeth pointing towards the handle. If the saw frame is held upright in a vice it will be found easier to 'thread' the veneer on to the blade, rather than to try to push the blade through the hole in the veneers (44). The other end of the blade is fixed in the frame and tightened. The correct tension of the blade is important, but is soon found by making a few practice cuts. The saw is released from the vice, the veneers placed on the cutting table, and sawing is commenced, keeping the blade moving steadily up and down in one spot while turning the veneer to keep the design line against the blade as cutting proceeds (45). When a sharp turn in the outline is reached, the saw should be kept moving without actually cutting, while the veneer is gradually turned until cutting can proceed in the new direction. If a corner is turned too quickly, or with the saw stationary, a broken blade is likely to result.

When the outline has been cut right round, the final strokes should re-enter the original needle hole, and the cut piece will drop out. The saw blade is released and removed from the veneer.

The flat bladed knife is now used to separate the cut out veneers and to remove the surplus veneer from the back of the picture (46). The

50

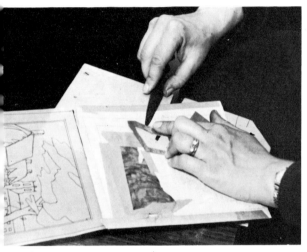
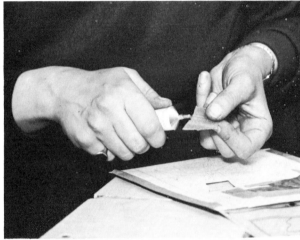

46 | 47
| 48

cut piece is then glued into place from the back of the picture by applying a little balsa cement to the edges (47 and 48). The same process is now repeated with the next piece of the picture. To save time, several pieces may be fixed to different parts of the picture at once, provided they do not overlap. They can all be cemented in place, left to dry for a short time, then cut out in the same order in which they were glued, and finally, when all the pieces have been cut out, they are separated and fixed in place, still in the same order, so that the cement is not over- or under-hardened on any piece.

It is often possible to save trouble and avoid having to cut an intricate line twice, by a little forethought in planning the cutting. For example, in the specimen design, if the sky veneer is to be cut in separately (the sky veneer not having been used as the waste veneer) it may first be inserted by using a simplified outline as shown in diagram 25, and can be cut in either by knife or fretsaw.

When the tree veneer has been chosen, the intricate outline between sky and tree only needs to be cut once. The two different ways already mentioned of making up the tree still apply, and the general sequence of stages in making up the design will be much the same as in the illustration already given. (26a, b and 32)

Certain parts of the picture may be more easily let in from the front of the picture than from the back. To do this, the veneer patch is cemented on to the face of the picture, with the outline traced on to it. The bevel cut must now be reversed, so that it is the upper veneer which is slightly oversized. This can be done by reversing the cutting direction, i.e. the veneer is now turned clockwise, so the saw follows the design line anti-clockwise. (49)

An alternative method is to have two slots cut in the angled cutting table as in figure 50. When letting pieces in from the front the cutting table is reversed, sloping downwards from left to right, and the cutting procedure is then unchanged. This method of inserting pieces from the front is especially useful when putting in the finer details of the picture, as it avoids the tendency for the downward pull of the saw to draw the patch away from the veneer.

It may sometimes be convenient, especially in a rather large picture, to assemble a certain section of the picture separately and then insert it into the background in one piece. Examples might be a boat, an animal, or a human figure, each of which might consist of quite a number of pieces of veneer. This section is traced on to a separate piece of waste veneer, and made up in the usual way, leaving a margin of at least $\frac{1}{4}$ in. on all outside edges. Meanwhile the main picture is also made up normally, again leaving an overlap on all the veneers adjoining

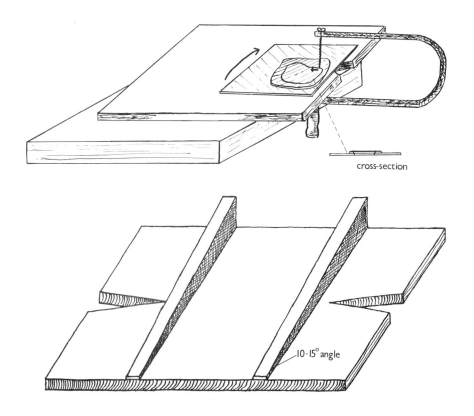

49 Method of cutting with veneer patch on top
50 Cutting table shown from underside

cross-section

10-15° angle

the separate section. The completed section is glued in place over the background, the exact outline traced on to it, and it is cut in from the front, as described above. (See also page 100.)

It is quite possible to make up a design completely using only the piercing-blade technique, but it is probably better to make use of the advantages of both saw and knife methods; the saw for taking the labour out of cutting brittle or hard veneers and long intricate outlines, and the knife for quickly cutting out simple background pieces, and for the insertion of the very finest of detail.

Before laying a picture cut by this method, the back of the veneer assembly should be lightly sandpapered to remove all traces of balsa cement.

53

7

The Baseboard

Once the cutting of the design is finished and it has been put away for a day or two it will be possible for you to take a fresh and critical look at it to detect any faults which can still be remedied before proceeding. In the meantime it is necessary to obtain a suitable baseboard on which to mount the picture, and to consider what kind of border or frame the picture will require.

TYPES OF BASEBOARD

Although invisible once the picture is finished, the baseboard is of great importance, since the correct or incorrect choice of board may well determine whether your picture will continue to delight future generations or will within a few months develop warping, splits, or cracks in the veneers which may necessitate its reluctant consignment to the dustbin.

Solid wood is particularly prone to warp, and so should never be used. The most suitable materials to use are plywood or laminboard, with blockboard as a possible, but inferior alternative. All of these are types of board constructed in layers to balance the various stresses exerted by the wood. Chipboard, too, is quite stable.

Plywood consists of layers of veneer of equal thickness bonded together, with the grain direction of succeeding layers at right angles. There is always an odd number of layers, so that the two outside sheets have the same grain direction.

Blockboard and laminboard consist of a central core of strips of solid wood, up to 1 in. wide in blockboard, 7 mm in laminboard, glued together with an outer face of good wood on each side, the grain running at right angles to the core strips. These boards have a similar overall appearance except when viewed from the edges, when the different forms of construction become apparent. They are available in different thicknesses, and the general rule is that the larger the picture, the thicker the baseboard should be.

For the very smallest picture, up to 4 in. × 3 in., $\frac{1}{4}$ in. thick board would be sufficient; $\frac{3}{8}$ in. thick for a picture up to 6 in. square, then $\frac{1}{2}$ in. for up to 10 in. × 8 in. and anything bigger should be on at least $\frac{5}{8}$ in. thick board.

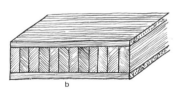

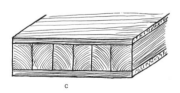

51a plywood
51b laminboard
51c blockboard

52

It is clear that any type of baseboard constructed so that different layers balance one another will be thrown out of balance again when the picture is glued on to one side of the board, and for this reason, as well as for the sake of appearance, it is always essential to veneer the back of the picture as well as the front. Otherwise the pull exerted by the veneers will eventually distort the baseboard and the veneers themselves will crack or lift.

As far as possible the extra layers added in veneering front and back should also conform to the right angles system of the baseboard. That is to say that if the preponderant grain direction of the woods in the picture is from side to side, the baseboard should be cut so that the grain direction of its outer layers runs up and down. Then the grain of the backing veneer should also run from side to side, and the stresses will again be evenly balanced so that there should be no danger of warping. The edges of the picture should also be veneered in order to hide the underlying baseboard. This is usually done with the same veneer as is used for the borders.

PREPARING THE BASEBOARD

The type and thickness of the baseboard having been decided, it must be cut exactly to the size required for the finished picture including borders, remembering to arrange the grain direction relative to that of the picture to be mounted, as mentioned above. The baseboard must be absolutely flat, and accurately cut, all the edges being at right angles to the flat surfaces and the corners exactly squared.

The surfaces and edges are roughened with a hacksaw blade (52), moving it diagonally across the grain in each direction to provide a good surface for the glue to hold. The baseboard is then ready for veneering the back, edges and front, which are normally laid in that order.

TYPES OF GLUE

There are several types of glue which may be used, and it is best to use one with which you are familiar. The three main types are:

1 *Hot glues*, such as Scotch glue, which are applied hot, and set as they cool under pressure.

2 *Cold glues* which harden by chemical action, taking a variable length of time, during which pressure must be applied.

3 *Impact adhesives* which stick on contact, without heat or pressure.

Scotch glue may be used for veneering large surfaces with plain sheets of veneer, but I would not recommend it for anyone not already experienced in its use. It is not very suitable for laying a picture as the glue may be drawn up between the veneers and discolour them. The application of heat and pressure also presents several problems.

Cold glues are more suitable, provided some means of applying pressure is available. As they do not set immediately the veneer can be eased into place and fixed in the correct position before the glue begins to set.

Impact glues are perhaps the least complicated for the beginner, as no press is required. The veneer must however be laid in exactly the right position, as once it has touched the baseboard it cannot be moved again. An impact adhesive is particularly useful for applying edge veneers and for veneering curved or irregular surfaces.

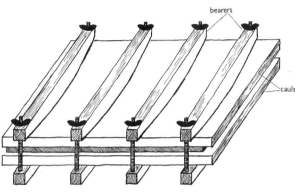

53 *Letter press*
54 *Home-made press*

If the marquetry assembly contains any materials such as metal, ivory or mother of pearl, or is being laid on to a surface other than wood, such as metal or plastic, the impact adhesive will still produce a firm bond, where most other adhesives are only suitable between wood surfaces.

PRESSES

If Scotch or cold glues are to be used, some means of applying pressure is essential. This may be simply a pile of heavy books, or two flat wooden boards with clamps, an old letter press, or a simple press especially made for marquetry. I know of one marquetarian who pressed his picture by jacking up his car and lowering the wheel gently on to the picture held between boards—however this method is hardly for general application.

The larger the picture, the more important it is to have an effective press. The old fashioned type of letter press with a central screw can sometimes be obtained cheaply at a sale of office effects (53) or a useful press can be made quite simply at home. (54 and 58)

An average sized press would be 15 in. × 12 in., but it can be made larger or smaller if required. Two flat pieces of plywood or blockboard of this size, and about 9 mm in thickness are required for use as cauls.

57

55

56

Four pairs of cross bearers, or three pairs for a smaller press, are cut from $1\frac{1}{2}$ in. $\times$ 1 in. hardwood, 2 in. longer than the width of the press. One of each pair of bearers is screwed to the bottom caul, equally spaced along its length and overlapping 1 in. each side of its width.

The top bearers should be shaped so that they taper slightly from the middle towards each end. The pressure can then be applied by G clamps, or if preferred the top and bottom bearers can be drilled to take bolts with washers and wing nuts. When the clamps or nuts are tightened, the shaping of the top bearers causes pressure to be applied from the centre of the panel towards the edges, which helps to squeeze out surplus glue and eliminate air pockets.

LAYING BACK AND EDGES

Collect together press, baseboard, glue, backing veneer and some newspaper and polythene. The backing veneer should be slightly oversize, overlapping the baseboard by about $\frac{1}{4}$ in. all round.

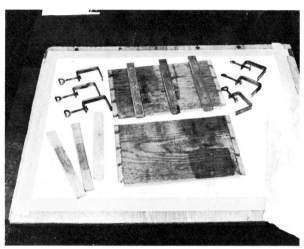

57

58

A thin even layer of glue is spread first on the baseboard, extending right to the edges, and a similar layer is applied to the backing veneer (55). After the required time, according to the type of glue being used, place the backing veneer flat, glued side upwards, and lower the baseboard down into position (56). If an impact glue is being used, take particular care to get it in exact position. Turn the baseboard over and work over the surface using the edge of a cork sanding block—or a veneer hammer if one is available. This is used from the centre of the panel in zig zag fashion, pressing the veneer down on to the baseboard and squeezing surplus glue towards the edges (57).

If cold glue is used omit the previous step. Check that the veneer is in the correct position; if it has slipped at all, with the veneer side downwards slide the baseboard on the veneer to the correct position. (Moving the veneer on the baseboard is likely to damage the veneer edges.) Cover the veneer surface with a sheet of polythene and several layers of newspaper, blotting paper or other soft material, and place

59–60

in the press, veneer side downwards (59). A few sheets of newspaper are put over the baseboard, and the top caul and bearers are placed in position. The central bearers are tightened a little first, then the outer ones, and then further pressure is put on until all the bearers have been fully tightened (60). Leave under pressure for 24 hours.

If a letter press is used, care should be taken not to apply excessive pressure. All that is needed is sufficient pressure to expel surplus glue, and keep the glued surfaces in contact. Further pressure will deform the veneer which may cause splitting later.

Even if impact adhesive has been used, it is advantageous though not essential to leave under pressure. The reason for placing the baseboard in the press with the veneer side downwards is that any surplus glue squeezed out will then collect on the overlap of the veneer and is removed when the veneer is trimmed. If the veneer is uppermost, the surplus glue runs down the edges of the baseboard, and will have to be scraped off.

When the baseboard is removed from the press, the surplus veneer is trimmed off with the knife (61) and then sandpapered flush with the edges of the baseboard. Strips of veneer are cut for the edges, slightly oversize both in length and width. The strips and the edges of the baseboard are glued, and the top and bottom edges should be veneered

61	62
63	64

first, using the impact adhesive (62). As soon as they have been pressed down into place, again using the sanding block or veneer hammer, the ends are trimmed to size (63) and the two side strips are laid in the same way.

After the glue has set firmly the ends are trimmed and the edges sandpapered flush with the surfaces of the baseboard (64). The reason for veneering the surfaces in this order is that the edges of the backing veneer are hidden by the edge veneers, those at the sides of the picture also hiding the ends of those at the bottom and top. When the picture itself is finally laid on the front, the whole border, back and sides of the picture can give the illusion of a solid block of wood.

An exception to the above order can be made if it is desired to have a fine contrasting strip round the edge of the picture as a feature of the border to be visible from the front. In this instance, back and front are veneered first, and the edges are put on last in a veneer of a contrasting colour. This can be particularly effective in a picture which does not have any other border.

(Recommended glues to use for laying include *Evostik Resin W* as a type of cold glue, and *Evostik Impact* or *Thixofix* as impact glues. It will be appreciated that it is impossible to consider the merits of all the many kinds of glues and polishes which are available, so only one or two brands of each type are suggested which have been well tried and found satisfactory up to the time of writing. New products are continually appearing however, and by following the various handicraft and wood-working publications and visiting 'Do it yourself' shops and exhibitions, information on interesting new developments in tools, glues, polishes and abrasives may be obtained, some of which may prove useful additions to the marquetarian's resources.)

SCREW EYES

If screw eyes are to be used for hanging the picture, they may be screwed in after polishing is completed. This is the simplest method. Some people however prefer to have them recessed into holes in the back of the baseboard, in which case the holes should be made at this stage. The base of the hole can then be covered with a small circle of the backing veneer before inserting the screw eye, as shown in the diagram.

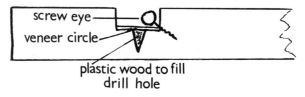

65 *Inserting screw eyes*

8
Borders

Not every picture requires a border. Sometimes if the picture consists of a portrait, or a motif such as a spray of flowers let into a suitable background veneer which extends to the edge of the baseboard, no border is necessary. Most other pictures however are set off to advantage by a framing border of contrasting veneer.

Highly figured and fancy veneers should not normally be used for the borders as they draw attention from the picture, and may even make it appear distorted. The best border veneers are straight grained, either of uniform colour or with a very faint stripe. Suitable examples would be sycamore, antaris or oak, for a light border; sapele or Nigerian walnut for a medium shade, and ebony or wenge for a dark border. However, figure 66 shows an unusual fancy border of matched walnut veneers, which is effective because of the plain background of the enclosed design.

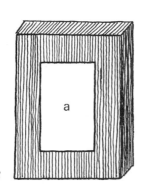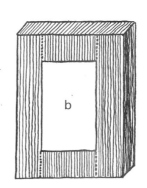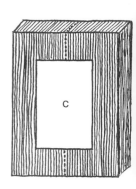

68

67

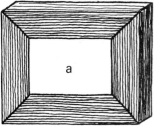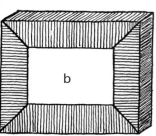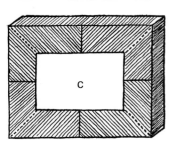

STRINGERS

A stringer, a narrow fillet of contrasting veneer, is often inserted between the picture and the border, and this is usually of a white veneer (sycamore or horse chestnut), if a medium or dark border is used. Occasionally a dark stringer is used with a light border.

TYPES OF BORDERS

There are several different ways in which borders may be arranged. The most usual type consists of four matching veneers of equal width with the grain direction running parallel to the sides of the picture, and the corners mitred (67a). Another type of border known as a 'cross banding' has the grain direction running at right angles to the sides of the picture; again the corners are mitred. This is very effective with a wood such as wenge which has a very close fine stripe (67b).

A further variation is to cut strips for the border at an angle of 45° to the grain direction. Like a cross banding this is most effective either in a closely striped veneer or one with a minimal grain marking. This can make an attractive border for a very small or fairly plain picture (67c). Usually if the borders have the grain running longways, the edges are also veneered long grain, while with a cross banding the edges are usually veneered cross grained.

Alternatively, the whole border may be cut, or can be made to

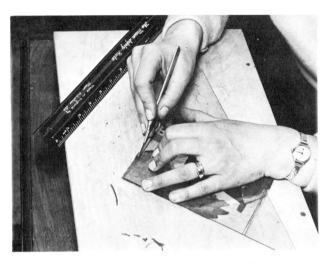

69

appear to have been cut, from a single sheet of veneer, with the grain direction running the same way in all four borders (68a and b). The illusion of a solid block of wood may be continued by cutting the edge veneers to match—long grain for the long edges and cross grain for the short ones, making the backing veneer to match also.

The borders may also be cut from a pair of matching veneers joined only at centre top and bottom. In a shadow-striped veneer like mahogany or Nigerian walnut, this gives a nice sense of balance to the picture with the sides exactly matching (68c).

SQUARING OFF

Before the borders are fitted, the picture must be trimmed to the correct size. It is important that it should be perfectly squared, otherwise the border mitres will not meet exactly at the corners of both picture and baseboard.

Using a steel straight edge, cut along the top border line through the picture and waste veneer. Then with a set square, the two sides are cut to a right angle (69) and finally the bottom edge is trimmed, leaving the picture ready for the borders. (If no borders are to be used, square off the picture leaving it slightly oversize—about $\frac{1}{8}$ in. all round—larger than the baseboard.)

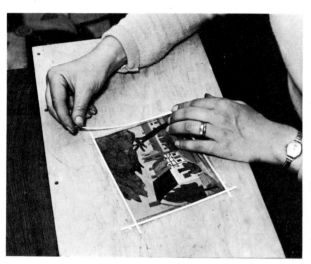 

70   71

If stringers are being used, they can now be put into position along the edges of the picture. They must be of exactly uniform width, and should be cut a little longer than the sides of the picture. They can be attached to the picture with tape or by butt jointing, leaving the ends overlapping (70). The corners are mitred by cutting across the intersection of the two veneers with a knife (71).

CUTTING BORDERS

If the borders are to be cut from matching veneers, that is to say four consecutive leaves from the same log, the four leaves should be numbered and placed in exact position on top of each other, using some feature of the grain or figure as a guide. They are taped firmly together, and a straight edge is put along the line of the grain and the four pieces are cut through together, using several cuts if necessary, but not allowing the pieces to move. The width of the border is measured and marked on the top veneer, allowing about $\frac{1}{8}$ in. to $\frac{1}{4}$ in. oversize, and the four pieces are again cut through (72a).

The top piece is attached to the top of the picture, and the second

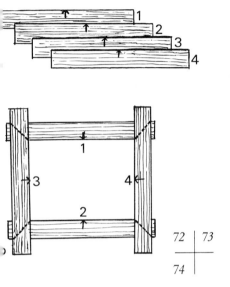

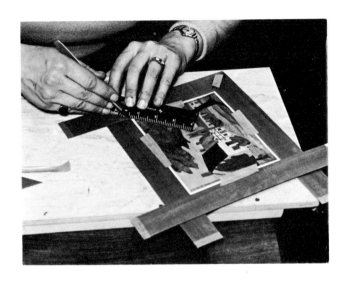

72 | 73

74 |

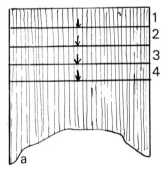

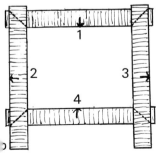

piece is turned over and attached to the bottom. The third piece is taped to the left hand edge and the fourth turned over and taped to the right hand edge (72b). The sticky tape should be put on from the front of the picture this time, instead of the back.

MITRING CORNERS

The four corners are then mitred. A straight edge is placed across from the corner of the picture to the point of intersection of the border veneers, and with the knife held absolutely vertically, the two veneers are cut through (73).

If a cross banding is being used the four borders can be cut from a single sheet of veneer (74a). To make the grain match well at the corners, the first piece should go at the top, the second down the left hand side, the third down the right hand side, and the fourth reversed across the bottom (74b). Before cutting cross bandings it is usually advisable to reinforce the veneer with gummed tape. The corners are mitred as before. N.B. With cross bandings, always cut away from the point when cutting the mitres to avoid splitting the veneer with the grain.

67

*75 The Dovedale Eagle
N. Douglas. Example of a
border made from four
matching veneers
76 The Haven
C. H. Good.
Example of cross banding*

LAYING THE PICTURE

The whole of the front of the picture is now covered with strips of sticky tape to hold it together (77). When this has dried out thoroughly the tape can be removed from the back of the picture by dampening it a little at a time and peeling it off. (78) Avoid using too much water. When all the tape is removed, leave the picture to dry, under a weight if necessary to prevent buckling.

Place the picture and border assembly face down on the table and position the baseboard on to it, matching the corners exactly to the border mitres. The borders having been cut oversize, the correct position of the baseboard can be marked with a pencil on the border overlap to help in locating it later.

Apply the glue to the baseboard and picture assembly, and when the glue is ready, lower the baseboard gently into its marked position (79), and work over the veneer surface as before (80). The rest of the

68

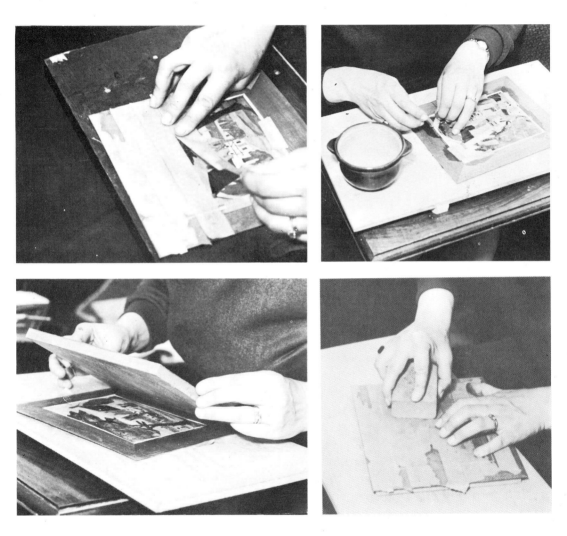

77 | 78
---
79 | 80

procedure for laying is as described in the previous chapter.

If using cold glue it is a good idea to remove the picture from the press after a few minutes to check that the veneer has not slipped—correct if necessary, then replace in press and leave for 24 hours. When the picture is removed from the press the surplus veneer is trimmed off and sanded flush with the edges.

9'

Finishing Processes

After the laying is completed, the picture should be left for a day or two to allow the glue to set really well. All gummed tape remaining on the face and on the edges of the picture is removed by moistening and peeling it off, and all the surfaces should be carefully examined to find any 'blisters', i.e. areas where the veneer is not stuck down to the baseboard. There are two ways of detecting them: firstly by running the finger tips lightly over the surface of the veneer, when a blister can usually be felt as a slightly raised area, owing to the air trapped underneath it; and secondly, by tapping the picture lightly all over with a finger nail or a knife handle. A hollow dull sound will be heard over a blister, quite different from that heard over the soundly glued veneer. If any blisters are found they should be dealt with at once by the methods which will be described in a later chapter. If this is not done, when the picture is sandpapered the blistered area, being above the level of the surrounding veneers, may easily be sanded right through, exposing the baseboard.

THE BENCH HOOK

During the ensuing processes of scraping, sanding, and polishing, a useful device for holding the picture is a 'bench hook'. This consists of a piece of wood or hardboard a little bigger than the picture being made, with a strip of 1 in. × 1 in. wood screwed to the underside of one long edge, and a strip of 1 in. × $\frac{1}{4}$ in. wood to the upper surface of the opposite edge.

The bench hook is placed flat on the table or work bench with the lower strip against the edge of the table (81). The picture bears against the upper strip which holds it in place, but, being thinner than the picture, does not interfere with the sanding block or polishing pad.

SCRAPING

This is not necessary for the back or edges where the veneer is of uniform thickness, but if there is considerable variation in the thickness of the veneers on the face of the work, the preliminary use of a scraper will reduce the amount of sandpapering required. A proper cabinet-

 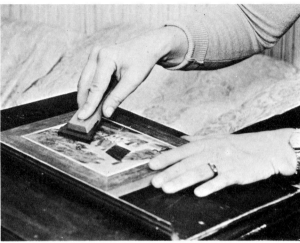

82

maker's scraper can be used, or a convenient substitute is a used safety razor blade, providing the edge is still reasonably smooth and sharp.

The scraper should be held so that the whole width of the blade is in contact with the veneer surface, and is tilted obliquely towards its direction of travel. As it is drawn across the surface of the wood it will remove shavings from those veneers which are raised above the level of the rest (82). It should be used in a series of straight strokes, concentrating on the thicker veneers. Do not allow the corners of the blade to dip, or try to clean up the surface of the thinner veneers. When the surface feels fairly level, the next step is taken, which is sanding. If the picture contains dyed veneers or certain brightly coloured natural veneers such as padauk, it is a wise precaution first to seal the grain of these and the surrounding lighter veneers individually with a fine paint brush and sanding sealer, to avoid coloured dust entering the pores of the adjoining veneers during sanding.

SANDING

A cork sanding block should always be used. Garnet paper is more satisfactory than glass paper for marquetry, and it is best to use three grades—4/0, 7/0 and 9/0. A coarser paper may level the picture more quickly, but at the cost of leaving deep scratches in the veneer which cannot be eradicated.

Using the 4/0 paper first, cut a piece to fit the sanding block, and begin to sand the picture in straight lines, either from top to bottom or side to side, according to the grain direction of the principal pieces of veneer (83). This is usually horizontal in a landscape picture, vertical in a portrait or flower study. Having decided which direction you will use, follow this throughout the sanding process. Do not allow the sanding block to dip over the edges of the picture, but end each stroke when at least two-thirds of the block is still flat on the picture, to avoid 'rounding' off the edges and corners. Stop frequently to brush off the sanding dust from the picture and from the garnet paper.

When the surface feels smooth and level to the finger tips, change to the next grade of garnet paper, and repeat the process, then change to the finest grade, and continue until the surface is clean and free from scratches. Finally, using a very old piece of the 9/0 garnet paper which has been rubbed almost smooth with previous usage, go over the surface again until it begins to take on a slight shine, the smooth paper having a burnishing rather than an abrasive effect.

When the surface appears to be perfectly smooth, lightly moisten a pad with methylated spirits, and wipe over the whole surface of the picture. This will bring out all the colours of the veneers and will also show up any imperfections in the surface. These must be attended to by further sanding, or they will show up even more when the picture is polished.

The back and edges are treated in the same way. Take care to keep the sanding block flat when sanding the edges to avoid bevelling them off.

SEALING

It is now necessary to seal the surface of the veneer, and for this purpose a 'sanding sealer' is used. This solution is brushed over the whole picture

and allowed to dry (84). This takes from $\frac{1}{2}$–1 hour. The back and edges must be treated similarly. In most of these processes it is convenient to treat the front of the picture and two opposite edges at one time, and the back and the other pair of edges the following time. When the sanding sealer is dry it forms a tough elastic coat over the surface, which must be then cut back by rubbing over with fine garnet paper. Several coats are applied in this way and sanded. Finish with a further coat, applied very thinly with a brush. This final coat is not sanded, and will protect the veneers from the chemicals present in certain types of polish which can affect the colours of some veneers such as harewood, green cypress and magnolia.

The effect of the sealing is to begin to fill up the pores in the grain of the coarser veneers. Certain veneers such as obeche and padauk, and burrs like elm, may require a good deal of filling. A transparent grain filler may be used, but in my experience this tends to show up as whitish spots in the pores of the darker veneers, and I prefer to have the grain filled first with sealer and then with polish, though this method may take a little longer.

TYPES OF POLISH

There are many different types of polish available, and the one chosen will depend partly on the purpose for which the marquetry article is intended. If it is a picture which will hang on a wall there is no need for the polish to be heat- or water-proof, but it should protect the veneers from discolouration due to dirt and dust. On the other hand veneered table mats, trays, coffee tables and such like, require a polish which is resistant to heat, water and spirit stains.

WAX POLISH

The simplest way of finishing a picture is with a plain wax polish, available for marquetry from handicraft shops. This is thinly applied with a soft cloth and then polished with a fresh cloth. Several coats will be needed, each being allowed to harden well before the next is applied.

Anyone acquainted with the Army method of 'spit and polish' for obtaining a high gloss on boots and belts will find the same technique useful here. A rag is wrapped over the index and middle fingers and a coat of polish is applied with it. Then the fingers, still covered with the rag, are dipped in water, and the polished surface is worked over in a series of small circles, remoistening the rag from time to time (85). This allows the polish on the picture to be smoothed down and burnished instead of being mainly reabsorbed by the polishing cloth. When the surface appears very smooth and shiny a light final polish is given with a dry duster.

Wax polish gives a pleasant glossy but non-reflecting surface. If several coats are applied a rich shine can be obtained and the wax fills the grain well. Its main disadvantage is that over a period of time it tends to become dingy and to attract dust because of the slight stickiness of the wax surface. To some extent this can be minimised by giving it an occasional rub with one of the silicone furniture polishes, such as *Pledge*.

An improved base for subsequent wax polishing is obtained by first applying two or three brush coats of 'Half and half' (equal parts of white french polish and methylated spirits) after sealing, rubbing down lightly after each coat, and finally applying wax polish as described above.

85

FRENCH POLISH

Detailed instructions for applying french polish can be found in many books and I do not propose to include them here. As a finish for marquetry work it has much to recommend it, giving an attractive deep shine which can be dulled down, if preferred, to a semi-matt finish. However, it is difficult to obtain good results with one's initial efforts at french polishing, so beginners would be well advised to use instead one of the newer types of 'home french polish' which are much simpler to use.

For those who are familiar with the use of french polish, there are one or two points to remember when applying it to marquetry work. Firstly of course, a white polish must be used instead of the tinted polish used for furniture, and secondly, linseed oil should not be used as a lubricant as this tends to cause yellowing of the light veneers. A colourless mineral oil such as liquid paraffin makes a good substitute.

If a gloss finish is required 'spiriting off' is carried out in the usual way but if a matt or eggshell surface is preferred, this is not necessary. Instead a final rubber of polish is used in straight even strokes the length of the picture, and continued until the rubber is barely damp, and begins to pull.

The picture should be left for at least a week for the polish to harden. Dulling down is then carried out with fine pumice powder, sprinkled on to a soft brush, and brushed in straight strokes across the picture until the required amount of dulling is obtained. For a very dull finish, the surface is first wiped with a damp cloth which causes the powder to cut more deeply.

'HOME FRENCH POLISH' (FURNIGLAS)

This is a method of french polishing which produces a similar final effect to that of a classical french polish, but has eliminated many of the difficulties and pitfalls. Full instructions will be found in the kit, which consists of a bottle of No. 1 polish, No. 2 solution for finishing, and 9/0 garnet paper for rubbing down.

A series of coats of polish are put on to the surface, using a pad of cotton wool wadding wrapped in a cotton or linen cloth. The film of polish dries very quickly, so that repeated coats can be applied, but no lubrication of the polishing pad is necessary, so there is no 'spiriting off' afterwards.

After each series of twelve or so coverings the work is allowed to dry, and then rubbed down with garnet paper. The object of polishing in this way is to fill all the crevices and pores in the wood without accumulating a great thickness of polish on the surface which would give a treacly appearance.

The final surface should be absolutely smooth and without blemish. When a sufficient depth of polish has been put on, and all the grain is filled, the No. 2 solution is used to remove the last traces of any marks from the polishing pad and bring out a high gloss. When buying the polish remember to get the white polish, and not the tinted version recommended for furniture.

OTHER POLISHES

The finish produced by the above process is good for a picture, but it is not very resistant to heat. For such articles of applied marquetry as trays, table mats, coffee tables, etc., *Furniglas Hardset* or *Rustins Plastic*

Coating is preferable. These produce a very brilliant surface which is resistant to heat, water, and spirit stains. Many people also prefer to use it on pictures as well, as it is absolutely colourless, whereas even the 'white' french polish or *Furniglas* has some yellow colouration still remaining.

The *Hardset* kit consists of polish and catalyst in separate bottles, marked to show the amounts of each to use, with a bottle of solvent, burnishing powder, and garnet and pouncing paper. Again full instructions are included, and I shall merely summarise here: A measure of polish and catalyst are mixed to make the solution to be used. Once mixed this has a limited life, as it gradually hardens, so only as much should be mixed as will be used in a few days. By keeping the mixture in a refrigerator while not in use, its life is prolonged considerably.

The preliminary layers of polish can be put on with a brush. Each coat should be allowed to dry for at least two hours, and then be rubbed down before applying the next coat. When the grain is filled and the surface level, a few final coats are put on with a pad. The film is extremely hard, and the final finishing processes with pouncing paper (or grade 400 'wet and dry' carborundum paper moistened with water) and then burnishing paste, entail quite hard work, but the result is rewarding.

Another type of polish which can be applied with a brush is clear *Ronseal*, obtainable in both gloss and matt finishes. A semi-matt or eggshell finish can be achieved by mixing the two. For a good result this must also be applied in several thin coats, not a single thick layer.

'SINKING'

Whichever type of polish has been used, it will be found after some weeks that the polish has 'sunk', so that the grain pores and the veneer joins in the picture show as slight depressions in the polished surface. At some time therefore, it will be necessary to sand the surface down once more with garnet paper until it is level, and apply a few final coats of polish and reburnish the surface. This procedure should not be carried out until at least two months after the original polishing;

the sinkage should then be complete, and this final polish should last indefinitely.

DULLING DOWN

One method of dulling down has already been described under french polishing, but most types of polish can be converted to a matt or eggshell finish which some people prefer, as it avoids reflections and allows the picture to be seen to better advantage.

It is not necessary to use a burnisher if the surface is to be dulled, but a perfectly even surface must first be achieved and any remaining brush or rubber marks removed by very light sanding with the finest pouncing or 'wet and dry' paper. Dulling down may be done either with pumice powder as already described, or with the finest wire wool, dipped in wax polish and drawn across the face of the picture in straight lines, in one direction only, until the required degree of dullness is achieved.

VARNISH

I mention varnish only to dismiss it as an unworthy finish for a piece of marquetry on which much time and labour has been spent. However carefully the varnish is applied it leaves a sticky finish which can neither be rubbed down nor burnished and which gives a cheap appearance to the work. The extra time involved in putting on a proper polish is amply justified by its durability and attractive appearance.

Whatever polish is used, remember that the back and edges of the picture should receive the same attention as the front, since the polish protects the veneer as well as enhancing its appearance.

10
Applied Marquetry

Traditionally, marquetry and inlay have been used much more as a means of embellishing furniture and other objects than as a purely pictorial form, and there is still much scope for the use of marquetry in making articles which are useful as well as decorative. A few such applications will be suggested here, but there are unlimited possibilities.

TABLE MATS

A set of table mats usually comprises four or six small ones about 6 in. × 6 in., two medium 8 in. × 6 in. approx., and one large one about 9 in. × 8 in., and may include a decorative stand to carry them. Obviously the dimensions are a matter of choice. A suitable base would be $\frac{1}{4}$ in. 5 ply, which should be veneered on the back and edges as for a picture. There are many possible ways of decorating the mats. Pictorial, floral, or geometrical motifs would all be suitable. If the designs were to be identical this might be an occasion for multiple cutting by fretsaw as described in Chapter 6.

Laying must be done with a glue which is really heat resistant. *Evostik Resin W* is suitable, and the same glue should be used for the edges which will need to be taped tightly in place to prevent slipping whilst the glue is drying. The finish chosen must be equally heat resistant, for example, *Furniglas* hardset. When completed the underside should be covered with baize or thin cork sheeting, cut slightly undersize.

TRAYS

The base of the tray is cut to size and veneered front and back in the usual way. The edges need not be veneered as they will be covered later. The surface should be sanded and polished before applying the moulding—again a heat resistant glue and polish are advisable. A tray moulding and a pair of handles can be obtained from a handicraft or 'Do it yourself' shop. The moulding must be mitred carefully to fit, and should be stained and polished before assembly. The frame is glued together, the mitred corners being reinforced with pins or by making saw cross-cuts across the corners and inserting pieces of thick veneer. If the frame is fixed to the base with screws rather than glue, it can be removed easily should it become necessary to repolish the tray.

86 Cocktail tray
Mrs H. Bridgland

TABLE LAMP

An attractive table lamp can be made by veneering a solid wooden base with a suitable design. It is also possible to make a lamp shade using sheets of veneer which, though not strictly marquetry, complements the marquetry base very well. The method is as follows: The veneers chosen for the shade should be straight grained, and free from any tendency to buckle. They should be attractive both in daylight and with a light shining through them. The frame to which they are to be attached should be only gently curved, and if the veneers are used with the grain running from top to bottom they can be curved to fit the shade without splitting.

The shade in the illustration was made by covering the ribs of the

87 Table lamp and shade
M. R. Campkin

frame with *Evostik* impact glue, and gluing a narrow strip of veneer about $\frac{3}{4}$ in. wide to the outside of each vertical rib. The six sheets of veneer were then glued on, so that the two edges were attached to the strips overlying the ribs, and the top and bottom were glued directly to the wire frame, overlapping it by about $\frac{1}{4}$ in. With *Evostik* it will be found that a strong bond is obtained even between the wood and the metal.

Narrow strips of contrasting veneer were inserted later on to the vertical gaps between the adjoining veneers, and finally the joints were reinforced by gluing strips of chamois leather about $\frac{1}{2}$ in. wide across the ribs and over the circular parts of the frame from the inside, gluing the leather both to the metal and to the veneer on either side. A possible improvement would be to line the frame with silk afterwards.

CLOCKS

A simple plaque made like a picture on a baseboard of $\frac{1}{2}$ in. plywood can make an attractive clock with the face decorated appropriately in marquetry, and a battery operated movement at the back. The movement and hands can be obtained through a handicraft dealer. A more elaborate clock can be made to enclose the movement in a case.

BROOCHES

Small brooches can be made in marquetry, with a design of a small picture, a flower, monogram, etc. The metal mounts, usually made of brass, oval or circular with a pin attached, can be obtained from the haberdashery counter of a department store where they are sold for making embroidery brooches.

Trace round the mount on to the veneer to be used as the background, and then position the tracing of the motif to fall correctly into the circle. When the design has been made up, the circle should be cut slightly oversize and glued in place with *Evostik*. A circle of the same veneer should be cut for the back with a slot cut out for the pin.

A small press can be made from two pieces of plywood 2 or 3 in. square, with a groove in one to accommodate the pin, and two clamps. The brooch is placed between layers of polythene, with some soft paper over the front, and left in the press for 24 hours. The excess veneer is trimmed and sanded down to the edges to the metal rim of the mount. The front and back are sanded and polished as usual, preferably with Hardset which is waterproof.

TABLES

Any kind of design may be used to decorate a coffee or occasional table, or a games table may be made with a chess board top. If the table top is fairly large it is best to use an impact glue, unless a large enough press is available. It may be found helpful to use the following technique to lay the top. The veneer assembly and baseboard are spread with glue and allowed to dry. A large sheet of brown paper is placed over the glued surface of the baseboard, and the veneer assembly is

88 Trinket box
3 in. × 2 in. × 1½ in.
C. Woodcock
89 Backgammon board
(reverse of figure 118)
M. R. Campkin

placed in position on the top of the paper. Neither glued surface will adhere to the brown paper which can be withdrawn gradually, so that the veneer is slowly brought in contact with the baseboard (i.e. the table top) and can be rubbed down a little at a time. This same method may be useful for a firescreen or a large picture.

A heat resistant polish should be used for the table.

BOXES

Perhaps the most popular form of applied marquetry consists of boxes in one form or another. They can be of any size and may be used for trinkets, cards and games, cigarettes and so on. An existing box of suitable shape may be covered with veneer, but it is more satisfactory to make the box for the purpose, and this need not be difficult.

The simplest kind of small box can be made from plywood or ramin about ¼ in. thick. Four pieces are cut for the four sides, making sure that all the corners and edges are square and true. The grain direction should be at right angles to that of the veneer which will cover the box. The four pieces are glued together with the shorter sides inside the longer, forming a frame.

Evostik impact glue may be used, or *Evostik Resin W*. The latter will give a stronger joint but the work must be clamped while the glue is drying. The top and bottom panels are cut to match the outside dimensions of the frame and are glued into place and the box is allowed to dry. All the surfaces are then sanded flush, and the box is veneered in this order: bottom first, then short sides, then long sides. The top will be veneered later. Again the box should be left for a day or two for the glue to harden.

Using a marking gauge, mark a line right round the box at the distance from the top where the lid is to come, usually about one-quarter of its depth. Use a knife and ruler to cut through the thickness of the veneer along this line.

Place the box in a vice with padding to protect the top and bottom, and using a small saw ('gentleman's saw') make a cut about 1 in. deep across each corner along the guide lines. Pack the other three cuts with veneer scraps while extending each corner cut in turn until the cuts almost meet, then finish off the cutting from the four sides until the lid is detached.

A sheet of 6/0 garnet paper is placed on a flat board or sheet of glass, and taped down along the edges. The two parts of the box are rubbed in turn on the garnet paper to smooth the cut edges. All four edges must be kept in contact so that they will be perfectly squared. When they are smooth, repeat the process with No. 9/0 garnet paper. The edges can be veneered either to match the outside of the box, or with a contrasting veneer if preferred; this will show as a stripe round the box when it is closed.

The design for the top is then prepared and glued in place on the lid. A block of wood placed inside the lid, and another on top with G clamps can serve as a press. Sand, seal and polish all surfaces in the usual way.

For a jewel or trinket box, linings are cut from $\frac{1}{8}$ in. plywood to fit inside the top, bottom and sides. These are covered with velvet or satin cut about $\frac{1}{2}$ in. larger all round and glued to the back of the lining plywood. The linings are then glued into place. For a cigarette box, linings of $\frac{1}{8}$ in. hardwood or plywood are cut and the edges mitred to fit inside the box. If the linings are made to project about $\frac{1}{8}$ in. above the rim of the box they will give location for the lid. A piece of baize

or leather may be glued to the underside of the box. (88)

As stated, this is a very simple type of box suitable for a beginner to try. Those with some experience of carpentry can improve on this by making the carcase of the box with dovetail or half-housing joints and adding hinges and locks. The glued joints described above are only suitable for a small box which will not be receiving any rough treatment.

If it is desired to put a design in marquetry inside the lid of the box, to show when the box is opened, it should be glued inside the top piece sanded, and polished, *before* the top is attached to the frame of the box.

85

91 Mah Jong pieces
M. R. Campkin

The whole of the inside of the box may be veneered, in which case all the veneer surfaces should be polished before the box is assembled.

A musical movement may be incorporated to play when the lid is raised. These are obtainable from handicraft dealers. Further possible applications of marquetry include book ends, fingerplates for doors, games boards (89) (see also under geometrical marquetry), firescreens (90) and so on. A name plate for a house is another possibility. This is made just like a picture but should be polished with a waterproof finish such as *Furniglas P.U.15*, exterior grade. Even then it would need to be in a sheltered position to prevent damage from damp.

Looking at the work of the craftsmen of past centuries in marquetry and inlay, one finds that they made use of a number of other materials besides woods, and that they also used techniques of bleaching, staining and dyeing woods in order to obtain special effects and increase the range of colours available.

The modern marquetarian has access to a larger variety of woods, with a greater colour spectrum, than the old craftsmen, so with some people it is almost a point of honour not to use any veneer which has been in any way artificially treated to alter its colour. However there are occasions when it may be appropriate to know some of these techniques of former days, or to make use of modern chemical dyes to achieve special effects.

SAND SCORCHING

The technique of scorching the wood with hot sand dates back at least five centuries. The inlaid choir stalls and cupboards in Italian churches are full of examples of the use of sand scorching to give an appearance of depth and roundness in the architectural designs and perspective *trompe l'œil* effects which they seem to have delighted in. Later, in the fine furniture of the seventeenth and eighteenth centuries, scorching was used to show the curves and shadows of flower petals and in the shells and scallops and geometrical motifs of Sheraton furniture.

In modern times it is still used with great effect, for example in the huge marquetry panels at Granite House; while on a humbler scale, it has enhanced many a smaller picture when used with discretion in a design of roses or other floral subjects.

The advantage of sand scorching is that it gives an even gradation of colour, fading from dark to light, seldom found occurring naturally in veneers. It can therefore be used to indicate a curved surface, such as a pillar with shadow on one side gradually giving way to light on the other; or a rose petal with a dark base becoming lighter towards the tip. On a human figure or face sand scorching can be used to indicate the curve of an arm or leg or the shadow of a muscle.

The technique is quite simple. All that is required is a small metal dish filled to a depth of about $1\frac{1}{2}$ in. with silver sand (obtainable from pet shops), a source of heat, a pair of tweezers or pliers to hold the veneers, and an old teaspoon.

The dish must be placed over a gas burner or electric hot plate until the sand is heated right through. This will probably take about 20–30 minutes. Once the correct temperature is reached it should be maintained as evenly as possible. The temperature can only be judged by repeated testing, using old scraps of veneer of the same type as that to be used for the picture.

A small piece of veneer, say about $\frac{1}{2}$ in. $\times$ 2 in., is held in the pliers and dipped into the sand to a depth of an inch or so, kept there for about five seconds, and then withdrawn and examined. As the sand is hottest near the bottom of the tin, and cools towards the surface, the shading will be darkest at the edge dipped into the sand and will gradually fade out towards the top. Do not allow the veneer to touch the bottom of the dish or it will char. If the shading is not deep enough dip the veneer again for a further few seconds.

If the sand is too hot the veneer will become blackened and brittle on the surface before the shading has penetrated through the thickness of the veneer, while if it is too cold the veneer takes so long to darken that it tends to shrink excessively in the process. (A small amount of shrinkage is inevitable owing to the drying out of moisture naturally present in the veneer.)

The correct temperature for the sand is usually that which will give a good depth of shading in 5 or 6 seconds. Darker or lighter effects can then be obtained by using a slightly longer or shorter time without risking either of the hazards mentioned above.

When the results on test scraps are satisfactory you can proceed to scorch the actual veneers for your picture. It is quite possible to do this by taking a piece of veneer larger than that required, scorching it, and then cutting the required piece from it using the 'window method' technique to get the shaded area as nearly as possible in the correct place. However, it is difficult in this way to get the shading to the exact shape required, so it is usually better to cut the piece first, and then scorch it to the exact pattern.

This can be done in two ways. Suppose the design is of a flower (92). Some of the petals simply require shading at the base. The piece for the

92 Rose Design

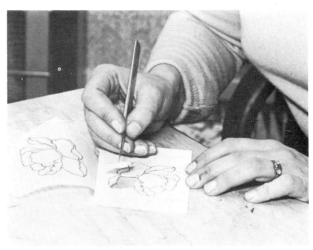

93
—
94

petal is cut to size from an appropriate veneer by the window method, making sure the grain of the wood is in the correct direction, as this is important even in a very plain veneer (93). The area of shading can be marked with a pencil. The piece of veneer is then held in the tweezers and the part to be scorched is dipped into the sand (94). Remember

95-96

that the upper quarter inch or so of the sand hardly marks the veneer, so make sure it is dipped in deep enough. After a few seconds check the shading and give it a little longer if necessary.

The completed piece is fixed back into the picture, and the next piece is cut out in the same way, shaded and inserted. Do not make the mistake of cutting all the pieces of the flower first so as to shade them one after the other, as you will find they no longer fit owing to the slight shrinkage which has taken place. By shading each piece and inserting it before cutting the next any shrinkage is allowed for as the adjacent piece is cut.

On some petals it may be necessary for the shading to follow a definite pattern which cannot be achieved simply by dipping. For this, a mask is cut from waste veneer to cover all of the piece except

that which is to be shaded. This is fixed tightly to the picture veneer with a piece of *Sellotape*. Holding the masked veneer in the pliers some of the hot sand is picked up with the spoon and poured on to the exposed part of the veneer, left for a few seconds and shaken off (95). This is repeated until the desired degree of shading is obtained.

If the area to be shaded is not of too difficult a shape, the mask may be dispensed with and the sand scooped on to the veneer at the appropriate place. If only a very small area is to be shaded the tip of the veneer can be dipped into a spoonful of hot sand instead of into the dish (96).

Remember to allow for the fact that the picture will later be sand-papered which will remove a little of the surface shading, so the shading should be fractionally deeper than the final effect desired. If in doubt, sand the piece lightly and moisten to see the effect.

DYED VENEERS

The use of dyed veneers in marquetry is fraught with hazards, and on the whole I think they are better avoided. In a picture made mainly from natural woods the pieces of dyed veneer tend to obtrude instead of blending with their neighbours. If dyed woods are used the key-word is *discretion*. A few small pieces, carefully chosen, may enhance the picture whereas large chunks of brilliantly dyed coloured veneers will probably ruin it.

Some colours which are not available in natural woods, notably bright shades of blue and green, are best avoided, and it may be better to change the time of day, or the season of the year, of the scene you intend to depict. It may be possible to make a pleasant picture by showing the same scene in the subdued lights of evening, or in the reds, browns, and yellows of autumn, where an attempt to indicate midday and mid-summer by the use of blue and green would be doomed to failure. Even dyed black veneers tend to look obtrusive, being darker and more uniform in colour than the darkest natural veneers.

As usual, however, the exception may prove the rule, and a number of people who had never had a good word to say for dyed veneers were forced to change their opinions a little by seeing a remarkable picture, *Freedom for Whom?*, in which the black curly hair of a negro warrior was shown to perfection by a piece of masur birch dyed black, where the variation in uptake of the dye by the softer and harder parts of the naturally mottled veneer resulted in most lifelike highlights and shadows (99). One thing I think this does show is that if you intend to use dyed veneers you are more likely to achieve satisfactory results by choosing and dyeing them yourself rather than by using the rather limited, rather lurid range of coloured veneers available commercially. These are usually dyed sycamore, so the grain pattern tends to be rather uniform and lacking in interest.

To dye your own veneers choose a few light coloured veneers of varying texture and grain pattern. Suitable ones include sycamore, obeche, maple and bird's eye maple and birch, but there is no limit to the possible experiments you can try. Use aniline dyes in powder form

made up with methylated spirits. Put half a pint of spirits in a glass container, which must have a screw top or other tight fitting lid.

The dye powder is sprinkled into the spirits and stirred with a piece of veneer of the type to be treated, and more powder is added until this veneer shows the desired colour. The pieces of veneer to be dyed are then immersed in the liquid together with one or two small spare pieces for testing. The jar is tightly closed and left for 72 hours.

The spare piece can then be taken out and broken across to make sure that the dye has penetrated right through, otherwise the colour will fade as the picture is sanded. If this is satisfactory the veneers are removed and rinsed under running cold water. The dye solution can be re-used as often as you like.

The veneers are laid on plain paper and left to dry. When they are almost dry they can be pressed if necessary to counteract twisting or buckling by laying them between sheets of clean dry paper, and placing under a weight.

HAREWOOD

Even those who dislike dyed woods often make use of harewood from time to time. This is produced by chemical treatment of veneers to produce various shades of grey, ranging from dark slate to bluish grey and silver, and is used in marquetry to depict stonework and sometimes for water effects.

Half a pound of sulphate of iron crystals are dissolved in a gallon of water. The veneer is put to soak in the solution for half an hour. It is then rinsed and dried. Any flat or open container serves for this purpose. If the solution is kept in a tightly closed container it can be used many times.

Only certain veneers respond to this treatment. These include sycamore, maple, ash, plane and birch. Oak will turn navy blue, and most other woods are not affected at all. Bird's eye greywood and grey lacewood are produced in this way from veneers of bird's eye maple and plane tree respectively, and these have interesting figuring which has many possible uses.

Masur birch also makes an interesting form of harewood, and its dark circles and patches can be used to good effect to indicate lattice or bottle glass windows in certain pictures.

The depth of colour depends on the nature of the original veneer and not on the length of time it is in the solution. Weathered maple or sycamore will give a darker shade of grey than plain maple or sycamore. Again it is a matter of experiment and trial and error.

BLEACHING

Oxalic acid crystals or ordinary household bleach may be used, but the results are rather unpredictable, and may not be satisfactory. If left too long in the solution or inadequately rinsed, the veneer may disintegrate, and as there are plenty of light coloured natural veneers there is not much advantage in using this process.

OTHER MATERIALS

Other variations from the use of natural veneers can include the incorporation into the picture or design of such materials as metal, ivory, tortoiseshell and mother of pearl. The scope is somewhat limited, and I think the average marquetry picture is not improved by such gimmicks as a mother of pearl moon, or an ivory clock face. There may, however, be occasions when it may be used attractively on a piece of applied marquetry, and again it should be used with discretion and artistic taste.

As these materials are all more difficult to cut than veneer, it is advisable to cut them to shape first and then let them into the veneer assembly by tracing round the outline, rather than treating them as a piece of veneer to be cut by the window method. Finishing may present some problems too as the surface of mother of pearl or brass might be scratched by the sandpaper, and it may be necessary to devise some means of protecting them.

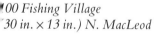

00 Fishing Village
′30 in. × 13 in.) N. MacLeod

12
Variations

Although any kind of picture can be cut by the 'window method' which has been described, there are a few additional techniques which may be used in producing special types of pictures.

SILHOUETTES

About the simplest possible form of marquetry picture is a straightforward silhouette of a single motif, for example an animal or flower outline, and this is one way for a beginner to make one or two simple pictures or designs for applied marquetry. Such a silhouette could be cut out by the window method, but an alternative method is to choose two contrasting veneers, preferably fairly straight grained and easy to cut. The two pieces are trimmed and squared slightly larger than the final size of the picture and taped together, the lighter coloured one uppermost. The design is traced on to the light veneer in the usual way, and the two veneers are cut together, keeping the knife exactly vertical all the time (101a). As usual, several light cuts are preferable to one heavy one, and any intricate parts of the design are cut with a series of pricks. When the cut is completed, the piece cut from the light veneer is inserted into the space in the dark one, and vice versa. In this way a pair of designs is completed simultaneously. Borders, if required, may be cut in one piece from the two veneers and interchanged instead of cutting separate borders and applying them afterwards (101b).

(This technique of cutting two veneers together may also occasionally be applied in cutting a part of an ordinary picture where there is a jagged or awkward outline between two pieces of a picture. Cutting the two adjacent veneers simultaneously avoids having to cut the difficult outline twice, i.e. once for the 'window' and once for the chosen veneer. This may also prevent some of the jagged points from getting broken off in the process.)

A more interesting silhouette picture can be made by finding or drawing a suitable skyline, perhaps with buildings, trees, or a group of figures, and using a dark veneer for the silhouette with an attractively figured veneer for the sky—for example, blue stained obeche for a daylight sky, or a reddish veneer for a sunset. The sky veneer should occupy the main part of the picture area to get the best effect of the

figuring. As this is not intended to produce a pair of pictures the cutting of the main outline can be done either by the window method or with the two veneers together, whichever seems more convenient. Any additional details can be cut in afterwards.

102 Summer Silhouette
7 in.× 5 in. M. R. Campkin
103 John F. Kennedy
Mrs J. Holmes

In *Summer Silhouette* (102), the veneers used were blue stained obeche and macassar ebony. (Dark walnut, if available, would be a much easier veneer to cut than ebony for this purpose.) The outlines of the grass, figures and tree trunk were cut through the two veneers together, but the leaves and branches were put in afterwards by the window method. Another application of the silhouette technique is illustrated by the portrait of President Kennedy which has produced an effective likeness with the use of only two veneers (103).

98

PORTRAITURE

Portraiture in marquetry can be an interesting and challenging variation from the usual type of design. Apart from the silhouette portrait already mentioned, a portrait can be tackled in the same way as any other design, using the usual range of veneers, but there are of course certain special problems to be overcome in order to achieve a good likeness and a life-like effect.

Faced with a photograph of the subject being attempted, the main problem is to divide up the face to show the different planes with their shadows and highlights. It is no good trying to use one large piece of veneer for the whole face and then adding the features afterwards—the result will remain uncompromisingly 'wooden'.

If possible a colour slide of the subject should be obtained; failing this a colour or black and white photograph will suffice. The slide should be projected on to a sheet of paper, attached to a cardboard backing, hanging on a wall, and the distance adjusted to give the desired size for the picture. All the outlines and details are then traced with great care, and in particular the areas of light and shade on the face should be defined as exactly as possible.

When the drawing is completed the paper is taken down, and then by comparing the drawing with the projected picture, the drawing can be shaded with a soft pencil to show the lighter and darker areas. The boundaries between the differently shaded areas should not be left as straight or curved lines, but should be drawn in a zig-zag fashion to correspond with the natural wrinkles or muscle lines of that area of the face; this will enable the different veneers to be blended in a naturalistic manner in the picture.

It is essential to have a good selection of appropriately coloured veneers from which to choose those for the picture. The type of veneers which may be useful for the face include pink pear, maple, ice or flame birch, masur birch, and sycamore. Remember to moisten the veneers when testing for colour, so that your shading will still be correct when the picture is polished. Texture is important as well as colour, and close grained veneers without too definite a figure are preferable, except where the figuring specifically contributes to a feature of the portrait.

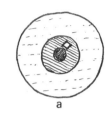

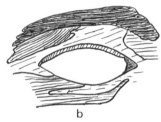

The portrait is traced on to a background veneer in the usual way. Although the features, eyes, ears and nose, are best cut in last of all, it is advisable to trace them on to the background at once, and keep retracing them when necessary as pieces of veneer for the various parts of the face are cut in, so that these veneers can be tried out and chosen in the context of the whole picture.

The grain direction of the veneers used must correspond with the natural lines of the face; running downwards on nose, jaw-line and neck, and across the forehead, cheeks and chin. If in doubt, a look at yourself in the mirror may help! The eyes are at once the most difficult and the most important feature of all, and are best left until last. To ensure that the eyes give the correct expression, and to avoid giving your subject an unwarranted squint, it may be found helpful to construct the two eyes separately on two pieces of waste veneer, making them circular showing the whole pupil, the iris with its usual highlight, and the white part of the eye cut as a circle surrounding the rest (104a). The two oval spaces between the eyelids of the portrait can then be cut out (104b), and the two 'eyes' placed behind them and adjusted until the correct effect is obtained, when they can be cut to an exact fit.

Although it is easiest to use a light coloured background veneer as a waste veneer for cutting the face by the window method you may wish the finished portraits to be on a different background. If so, after completing the portrait it can be separated in one piece from the surrounding waste veneer, laid on the chosen background veneer, and the outline carefully cut round so as to insert the portrait into the new background.

The three illustrations, 105, 106 and 107, show different styles of portraiture by three members of the Marquetry Society.

The same general principles can also be applied in making a detailed animal study (108).

LARGE PICTURES

When working on a very large picture or perhaps a design for a fire-screen or coffee table, it may be found rather awkward to do intricate cutting especially in the upper part of the design, where one is faced

104 Method of putting eyes in portrait

100

105 A Moroccan Jewish
Immigrant
A. Ephrat, Israel
106 Ken Dodd
N. A. Douglas (detail)

107 Early American
H. R. Quick (detail)
108 Cocker Spaniel
A. Guglielmo, U.S.A.

109 Method of breakdown into smaller areas of large picture shown in fig. 100, p. 95

with the alternative of working at arm's length leaning over the rest of the picture, or else turning it round and working on it upside down. Under these circumstances it is usually preferable to work on smaller sections of the design separately. The main large pieces of veneer such as sky, fields, water or roads are put in first as usual, then a section of the picture with a fairly straightforward outline such as a group of buildings, or a boat, an animal or human figure can be traced on to a separate small piece of waste veneer, and cut out by the usual window method. When completed this whole section can be detached from the waste veneer and cut into the appropriate part of the main picture. It is usually possible to complete quite a large proportion of the picture in this way, leaving only a few final details to be put into the complete assembly (109).

MINIATURES AND FINE DETAIL CUTTING

From the largest pictures to the smallest—the Marquetry Society defined a miniature, for competition purposes, as a picture with an overall area not exceeding 12 sq. ins. There is no basic difference in the general method, but a small picture needs a considerable amount of fine detail cutting to give it interest. The techniques of putting in the small detail can often be equally useful in a normal sized picture.

The choice of veneers for the parts of a miniature demands a slight alteration of viewpoint. In the ordinary way, for example, if one were

depicting a lake or river, the piece of veneer might be perhaps 5 in. ×
2 in., and a veneer would be sought in which the figuring would give a
suggestion of ripples or currents. In a miniature, however, the piece
of veneer might be only $\frac{1}{2}$ in. × $\frac{1}{4}$ in., yet it is still necessary to find
something to look like water. In this case it is not bold figuring on the
veneer which is sought, but the pattern of the individual grain pores
which can be used to suggest the desired effect.

Hairlines Very fine lines, just the thickness of a knife cut, are sometimes needed to depict rigging on ships, thin branches on trees, lattice
windows and so on. If the line is to be really thin, it is not necessary
to cut any veneer out of the background, but a cut is made with a knife
along the line, making sure it goes right through the thickness of the
veneer. Choose a straight grained veneer for the wood to be inserted
and with a straight-edge and a knife, cut a few straight thin splinters of
the wood along the grain line, until you have a suitable one. Using
the handle of the knife smooth the splinter to make it quite flat. Insert
one end into the background veneer, sliding it to the end of the cut,
and gradually press the splinter into the cut, trimming off any excess
at the other end. Press the splinter well down with the back of the knife,
then rub a little glue with your finger along the line. The glue causes
the splinter to expand a little giving a tight fit. If the line to be inserted
is curved it may be found helpful to curl the splinter before inserting it
by drawing the back of the knife along it from end to end.

Grass It is possible to give a suggestion of grass simply by putting in a
piece of magnolia veneer, which is a good colour, but a far better
effect will be achieved by superimposing on this background a number
of individually cut blades of grass. This is not as difficult as it sounds.
The main outline of the grass area is filled by a piece of magnolia, then a
series of pointed pieces are cut out, the first ones overlapping the
adjoining veneer above. The pieces should have a narrow point but
can widen towards the base. Corresponding pieces are cut from the
magnolia veneer, using different areas of the veneer to get slight
variations of colour. It is *not* necessary to cut these pieces exactly to
size so long as the point is approximately right. The point is touched
with glue and inserted into one of the spaces, and the base can be

*110a Grass (from miniature
figure 23a)*

roughly trimmed. Further points are cut out of the background in the same way, overlapping those already inserted, and more pieces are put in. By working on different parts of the area to be covered in turn, time is allowed for the glue to dry in one spot before a further piece is cut out from there. Several rows should be put in like this, with the tips a little lower each row. Finally the bottom edge of the 'grass' is trimmed to size so that the adjoining piece beneath can be cut in. This method was used in the miniature picture *Cotswold Village* (23a. Details 110a, b).

Trees One method of representing trees in miniature is also shown in the same picture. Three or four veneers or burrs of slightly different colours were chosen, and from each one was cut two or three straight narrow strips, which were then cut diagonally into diamonds. After putting in the veneers for the trunk and main branches of the tree, small diamond shaped holes were cut out round the branches, cutting them to size simply by eye, and fitting in the diamond pieces with a spot of glue. Again by working in several areas in turn, overlapping the diamonds already cut, and mixing up the different shades of the veneers quite a realistic effect can be achieved in a remarkably short time (110b).

STRINGERS

Because of the small size of the stringers and borders for a miniature picture I find it best to lay the picture first by itself, trimming and squaring it after it has been stuck down.

For stringers one method is to cut narrow strips of veneer and glue them standing edgeways so that it is the thickness of the veneer which forms the stringer. After the borders have been laid the superfluous veneer above the surface can be trimmed and sanded level.

Another method is to lay stringers considerably wider than required, then when they are stuck down, trim them to the desired width and remove the surplus. Borders can then be added.

110b Trees (magnified four times)

110c Billy Budd
M. R. Campkin

111 Stands

STANDS

A miniature picture usually requires a stand to support it. This can be made from a piece of plywood cut to shape, veneered to match the picture, and glued on the back. (111a)

Alternatively an attractive stand can be made from an old spectacle frame by detaching the hinge, cutting the ear piece to a suitable length, and gluing or pinning the hinge into a recess cut in the backing veneer at the appropriate place. (111b)

13

Geometrical Marquetry

In geometrical marquetry, patterns are made up of geometrical shapes—squares, diamonds and triangles. This form of decoration, which is known as parquetry, was used a good deal on furniture in the eighteenth century, and it is still a useful way of decorating applied marquetry as it is quickly and easily made up, and at the same time can be attractive and interesting.

THE JIG

A special jig is necessary which is made from hardboard or plywood as in the photograph. The two strips of wood must have true edges and the angle must be exactly 60°. If desired, a bench stop may be fixed on the underside, but this is not essential.

The knife used can be a little heavier than that used for pictorial marquetry. I use a No. 3 Swann Morton handle with a 23 blade. Two or three straight-edges of different widths are also required—a hacksaw blade and a steel ruler will do to begin with (112).

VENEERS

The best veneers for geometrical marquetry are straight grained, easy to cut and with little or no figuring. Suitable light veneers for this purpose include horse-chestnut, sycamore, obeche, avodire and birch; medium shades, cedar, African walnut, sapele, harewood; and dark shades, mansonia and dark walnut.

The chess board illustrated was made from horsechestnut and dark mansonia.

CUTTING BASED ON A SQUARE

The simplest pattern is of contrasting squares as for a chess board.

A sheet of straight grained veneer is chosen, one edge is trimmed with the grain to a true straight edge, and this is placed against the jig stop. The ruler is placed over it, pressing against the jig stop, and the veneer is cut along the ruler, using several light cuts if necessary. This strip is removed, the veneer and ruler are pushed up to the jig stop again and a

further strip is cut in the same way (113). An equal number of strips are cut in the same way from each of two contrasting veneers. The strips are then taped together with gummed paper tape, with the two colours alternating (114). Using a right angled set square placed over the sheet of veneer against the jig stop, one end of the veneer is trimmed exactly to a right angle (115). This end is now placed against the stop

107

116|117
118

and strips are cut as before (116). Each strip now consists of alternate dark and light squares, and when alternate strips are reversed and taped together a draughts board pattern is the result (117). This may be used to make a draughts board by assembling a sheet of 8 × 8 squares of suitable width (about 1½ in.) and mounting it with stringer and borders on to a baseboard in the same way as for a picture (118). Alternatively it may be applied to a table top to make a games table or a small version may be made and fitted inside a box for a travelling chess set.

However, the pattern of squares may also be used to make further patterns. Taking a straight-edge, cut diagonally across the dark squares from point to point (119). If each new strip of veneer is then moved along half a square a zig-zag pattern is formed (120). The light squares are then also cut diagonally, and the strip moved half a square along, giving a pattern of chevrons (121). If alternate strips are reversed a pattern of triangles emerges (122).

Several variations can be obtained by rearranging the strips in different ways. The strips can be taped together in any of these patterns, and then the sheet so made can be turned and the strips cut across the opposite diagonals to obtain a new series of patterns.

108

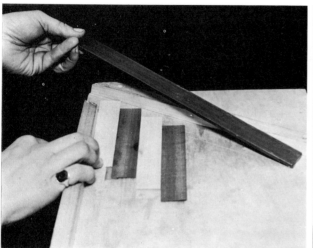 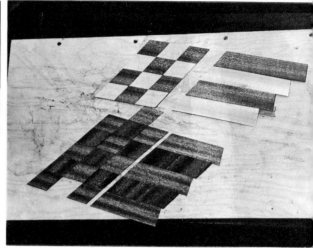

PATTERNS BASED ON DIAMONDS

For these patterns the angled stop is used; a hacksaw blade is a convenient width. Strips of two contrasting veneers are cut as before and taped together, with the ends stepped as shown to avoid waste (123). The side of the sheet is placed against the straight stop with its end touching the angled stop. The straight edge is put against the angled stop and the veneer is cut through. This piece is discarded. The veneer and straight edge are pushed against the angled stop again, keeping the straight side tightly pressed against the straight stop, and a further strip is cut, and so on. These can be arranged to give a pattern of diamonds. This can be particularly attractive if instead of using two contrasting veneers the same veneer is used, in strips cut with the grain, and strips cut using the jig at 60° to the grain direction. The resulting pattern gives a woven effect which is like that sometimes seen on old marquetry furniture (124).

Returning to the contrasting pattern; the strips of diamonds can be reversed and rearranged as described for the square patterns. They can be taped together and then cut across the points of one row of diamonds. If this cut edge is placed against the angled stop and strips cut off with the same straight edge, it should be found that all the diamonds will be

110

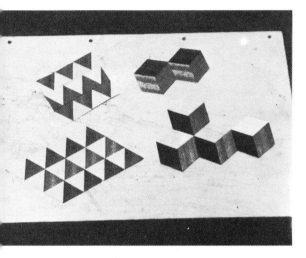

25 Different geometrical
patterns based on diamond
26 Small chest of drawers,
veneered with Cube pattern
A. R. Campkin

bisected, giving a pattern of triangles. This is a good test of the accuracy of the cutting. These strips too can be reversed and rearranged for further effects.

A further variation is the use of three contrasting veneers to form the 'reversing cube' pattern which is sometimes seen on old furniture and Tunbridge Ware articles. For this, strips of three contrasting veneers are cut. Without taping them together this time, each strip is placed against the angled stop and a series of individual diamonds are cut off. These are arranged as shown, to form a pattern which gives the optical illusion of cubes which appear to face in two directions. This is most effective if the two veneers representing the sides of the cubes are of rather similar colour (or the same veneer can be used with the grain in different directions) and a contrasting veneer used for the top or bottom of the 'cubes'.

USES OF GEOMETRICAL MARQUETRY

The patterns made by these methods can be used in many ways; to decorate table mats, trays, bookends, etc. They can be made to any scale, and used to cover a small area or a large one equally well.

14

Faults and Remedies

Throughout the previous chapters I have tried to show how to avoid faults in cutting, laying, and finishing marquetry work, but since, despite all precautions, accidents occasionally happen, this chapter is concerned with ways of repairing the damage as far as possible.

CUTTING FAULTS

False cuts   Sometimes when cutting out a 'window', the knife may slip and cut an adjoining veneer leaving a mark which, if left, will become increasingly obvious, especially on light veneer, as the cut fills up with dirt, glue, sanding dust and polish. As soon as a false cut has been made, place a drop of water on the veneer over the cut. This swells the fibres and if the false cut is with the grain, it will virtually disappear.

If it is across the grain, use the point of the knife to make several tiny scratching strokes *with* the grain fibres, *across* the false cut. This has the effect of raising some of the grain fibres on either side and pressure with the knife handle from either side towards the cut will interlock them across the cut. Then cover the place with a small piece of gummed tape.

If the false cut has gone through the whole thickness of the veneer, the same treatment is applied to the reverse side as well. To avoid dirt getting into the cut, the gummed tape is not removed until the picture is ready for sanding, when it will be found that the cut is quite unobtrusive.

False cuts are most likely to occur:
1 When cutting a rather tough veneer with a blunt blade.
2 When cutting towards, instead of away from, the apex of a pointed feature of a design.
3 When using a straight-edge. This is hardly ever necessary in a picture, but when it is essential, cut from each end towards the middle of the line to be cut, to avoid over-running into the adjacent veneer.

Bad joins   When the cutting of the design is complete, it may be found that there are one or two bad joints between the pieces. Where possible this should be corrected by re-cutting one or other of the adjoining pieces; but sometimes this may not be feasible if both form important features of the picture, or a suitable substitute veneer is not available.

If the bad join is along a fairly straight line, for instance between the sky and the horizon, choose the veneer in which the line runs with the grain—if both do, choose the darker of the two veneers. Try to find the actual sheet of veneer from which the piece was cut, and cut a few straight slivers along the grain from as near as possible to the source of the original piece. When you have a piece of the right size, turn the picture over, and working from the reverse side, first scrape out any glue from the gap without enlarging it. Press the sliver into place with the back of the knife very firmly; it should be a tight fit, but trim if required. Finally, rub a little glue over the join with your finger and this will penetrate sufficiently to hold the piece in place. From the front, the piece inserted will not be noticeable.

When the bad join is on a curve or angle, it is a little more difficult to rectify. If one of the adjoining veneers is a burr, the gap may be filled with a sliver of the same burr if carefully chosen, as the wild figuring helps to disguise the inserted piece.

If both veneers are straight grained it may be possible to cut out the part with the bad join by splitting one veneer along the grain, and replacing it with a new piece of the same veneer with the grain direction carefully matched so that the junction is along the line of the grain (127a and b). Where the gap cannot be patched unobtrusively in any of these ways, it may be preferable to enlarge the gap to an appropriate shape, depending on its place in the picture, and cut in a definite piece of suitable veneer to look in context with the rest of the picture rather than to put in a small piece which remains conspicuously a patched up job (128a and b). (Both these examples are taken from the design shown in figure 24.)

113

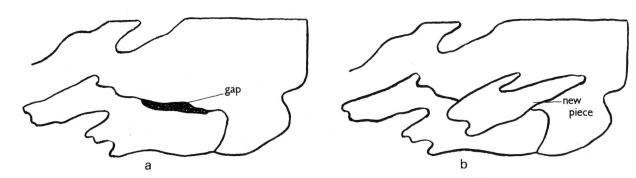

a   b

128a and b Correcting cutting faults

Small natural faults in the veneers, particularly in burrs, can also be dealt with in one of the above mentioned ways.

BLISTERS

As was mentioned in the chapter on finishing processes, it is important to detect and deal with any blisters before commencing sanding.
Blisters may be caused by :
1   Inadequate, excessive or uneven application of glue. Glue should always be spread thinly but evenly on both surfaces. (*Evostik Resin W* is an exception, the makers recommending application to one surface only.)
2   Failure to apply adequate heat with Scotch glue; inadequate pressure with cold glue, or inadequate rubbing–down with impact glue.
3   The use of incompatible glues for butt–jointing and laying. For example, traces of balsa cement used for butt–jointing remaining on the underside of the veneer could prevent the bonding of veneer to base-board in these areas with certain other types of glue. Balsa cement appears to be compatible with Scotch glue, but a white PVA glue is more suitable where laying is to be done with a cold or impact glue.

(Problems can also arise due to incompatibility between glue and polish; for example, if PVA glue has been used for butt–jointing, and ordinary french polish is later applied, it appears to dissolve out the glue resulting in excessive sinkage in the veneer joins, which does not occur if, for example, balsa or clear glue has been used.

It is clearly impossible here to give all the possible combinations of

114

glues and polishes which are or are not compatible. If in doubt, experiments with odd veneer scraps may solve the problem, or information can be sought from the manufacturers of the products concerned.)

Treatment of blisters   Scotch glue and some other glues can be remelted by the application of heat over the blister, working from the edge of the blister towards the centre. This may be done with a soldering iron or the tip of a domestic laundry iron, taking care not to apply them too hot. Another method is to use the flat end of the head of a hammer, heated by immersion in boiling water for a few minutes. As soon as the glue begins to soften pressure must be applied to flatten the blister and the glue is then allowed to reset. Too much heat will begin to raise the surrounding veneers.

If there is insufficient glue under the blister, a little more must be introduced. This is done by making a small slit in the blister with the point of the knife, splitting the veneer *with the grain*. A little glue is then pushed in with the knife blade through the slit, and pressure is applied to spread the glue and flatten the blister. The slit will then disappear. This method may also be used where the glue used originally cannot be remelted with heat.

For a more extensive blister it may be possible to prize out the whole affected piece of veneer, scrape off the dried glue from the underside and the baseboard, and glue the piece into place again. Pressure can be applied by clamping a small block of wood over the affected area, using a G clamp if it is near enough to the edge of the picture, or using a pair of bearers and clamps if it is nearer the centre.

If the piece cannot be removed intact, or where a piece of veneer has been sanded right through because of an undetected blister, the whole piece must be removed and replaced. To do this, first cut round the outline carefully with the point of the knife; then make a slit across the middle of the veneer, slide the knife blade in and ease the pieces out from the middle towards the edges. (Levering them out from the edge will bruise the adjacent veneer.)

Place a piece of paper over the gap in the picture, and rub over it with a soft pencil to obtain an exact outline of the missing piece. This can then be traced on to a suitable piece of veneer, and a new piece cut.

This method may also be used if for any other reason it is necessary to replace a piece of a picture after it has been laid.

DENTS

A dent may be due to excessive pressure having been applied in one spot in laying or it may occur accidentally if something is dropped on to the work. To treat it, put a drop of water on to the depression, cover with a piece of paper and press gently with a warm iron, taking care not to apply so much heat as to soften the glue. The water causes the veneer fibres to swell, and the warmth draws them up to the surface.

If a dent occurs after polishing, the polish on the affected area must be removed before the dent can be treated.

RESTORATION

Several of the above techniques may be found useful in the restoration of damaged veneered furniture. Most old furniture has been glued with Scotch glue so that blisters and loosened veneers can fairly easily be relaid by the application of heat.

Damaged or missing inlays can be replaced by carefully matching the veneers, and cutting to shape as described above. If necessary the piece could be sand scorched or tinted according to the nature of the missing piece.

It is usually necessary to strip off the old polish before carrying out these repairs and the whole piece of furniture will then need to be re-polished. Older furniture which has never been french polished should not be stripped, but the repaired area and surroundings should be treated with linseed oil, followed by wax polishing to match the original surface.

29 Completed picture from
figure 24

The Marquetry Society

This book embodies much of the collective experience of the members of the Marquetry Society, which was founded in 1952 to promote interest in marquetry as a hobby and as an art form. By arranging lectures, demonstrations and competitions and through its Journal, the Society encourages its members to attain the highest standards of artistry and craftsmanship.

The Society now has around eight hundred members, mainly in Britain but also in many other parts of the world, who receive the quarterly journal, *The Marquetarian*, which contains articles and photographs on all aspects of the craft. There are 20 active Groups of the Society throughout the country, each with its own programme of meetings and competitions, and individual non-Group members are enabled to make contact with others.

A National Exhibition is held annually, hosted by each Group in turn, and all Society members may send entries for competition. Further information about the Marquetry Society may be obtained from the Hon. Gen. Secretary, Mrs P. M. Aldridge, 2a The Ridgeway, St Albans, Herts., AL4 9AU, England.

Reference books

The Marquetarian Journal of the Marquetry Society Issues 1–59 (1952–67) *Marquetry* Atlas Handicrafts Leaflets *Intarsia and Marquetry (1903)* F. Hamilton Jackson *Marquetry and Veneers* K. Kitson (Foyles Handbooks) *The Veneer Craftsman's Manual* W. Lincoln (The Art Veneers Co. Ltd) *Wood Technology* W. Lincoln (The Art Veneers Co. Ltd) *The Fascination of Marquetry* Clifford Penny *The Craftsman in Wood* Edward H. Pinto

Supplies

Veneers and all other requirements for marquetry may be obtained by mail-order from the Art Veneers Co. Ltd, Industrial Estate, Mildenhall, Suffolk, and Abbey Marquetry, 28 Rose Walk, St Albans, Herts., AL4 9AF.

The *Veneer Craftsman's Manual* contains an extensive catalogue of these items, together with extracts from the articles from *Woodworker* magazine mentioned above, and is available by post direct from the Art Veneers Co. Ltd.

All the glues, polishes, abrasives and tools mentioned in this book are obtainable from most Hardware or 'Do-it-yourself' stores; and marquetry kitsets are also widely available.

Index